Praise for *Coming Out of Homosexuality*

"Coming Out of Homosexuality has much to say to both those
who think leaving homosexuality is something that can be easily done
and those who reject the possibility of it altogether. Through
research and testimony, Davies and Rentzel convincingly show that
God's power, though not immediately realized, is by no means
impotent in healing the homosexual soul."
Stan Jones, *Christianity Today*

"For the person who has been walking through the desert of homosexuality,
this book is going to be like a refreshing drink of water. I recommend it."
Rich Buhler, *author and host of the*
nationally syndicated radio program Table Talk

"This book is reassuringly frank, asking (and answering) the hard questions.
I think it will be enormously helpful to Christians struggling with
homosexuality and to those who seek to understand and encourage them."
Tim Stafford, *author*

"Coming Out of Homosexuality offers the reader far more than
a vague hope of healing. It takes the issue of homosexuality by the scruff of
the neck and offers realistic expectations to those in the process of overcoming their sexual difficulty. The book presents honest and practical advice
to those men and women who want to move from the plateau of being and
"ex" anything onto the highway of embracing their full identity in Christ."
Jeanette Howard, *Reconciliation Ministries*

"The book . . . has dozens of practical and realistic suggestions
for helping people change."
Christian Counseling Today

"One can only wish that this book had been written decades ago to give
practical scriptural guidance on how to come out of homosexuality.
The book blends compassion and realism, warnings and hope. I will highly
recommend this book to those who struggle with homosexuality
and despair of finding their way out."
Erwin W. Lutzer, *Moody Church*

D0368338

COMING OUT OF HOMO- SEXUALITY

New Freedom
for Men & Women

Bob Davies & Lori Rentzel

With Questions for Individuals
or Groups

INTERVARSITY PRESS
DOWNERS GROVE, ILLINOIS 60515

InterVarsity Press® is the book-publishing division of InterVarsity Christian Fellowship®, a student movement active on campus at hundreds of universities, colleges and schools of nursing in the United States of America, and a member movement of the International Fellowship of Evangelical Students. For information about local and regional activities, write Public Relations Dept., InterVarsity Christian Fellowship, 6400 Schroeder Rd., P.O. Box 7895, Madison, WI 53707-7895.

All Scripture quotations, unless otherwise indicated, are taken from the HOLY BIBLE, NEW INTERNATIONAL VERSION®. NIV®. Copyright © 1973, 1978, 1984 by International Bible Society. Used by permission of Zondervan Publishing House. All rights reserved.

The stories in this book are based on the lives of real people. In cases where first names only are used, names and identifying details have been altered to protect the privacy of the individuals involved.

Cover background painting by Robert Linkiewicz

ISBN 0-8308-1653-4

Printed in the United States of America ∞

Library of Congress Cataloging-in-Publication Data

Davies, Bob, 1951-
    Coming out of homosexuality: new freedom for men and women/Bob
    Davies & Lori Rentzel.
        p.   cm.
    Includes bibliographical references.
    ISBN 0-8308-1653-4
    1. Homosexuality—Religious aspects—Christianity.   I. Rentzel,
Lori, 1953-   . II. Title.
BR115.H6D38   1993
248.8—dc20   93-41902
                                                    CIP

17   16   15   14   13   12   11   10   9   8
07   06   05   04   03   02   01   00   99   98   97

Dedication

To Frank Worthen,
founder of Love In Action
and a pioneer
in the ex-gay movement.
Frank, your life has been
an inspiration to countless men
and women around the world.
Thanks for leading the way.

Acknowledgments

We give sincerest thanks to the whole team who made this book possible: to Becky Cain, for countless hours of transcribing taped interviews and also babysitting Lori's children while Mom went to the library to write; to Pam Davies, for her steadfast support throughout the entire two-year writing process; to Rudy Rentzel, for his helpful observations and late nights watching the kids; to our IVP editor Cindy Bunch-Hotaling, for her enthusiastic support and expertise from the moment we signed the contract; to Carol Gulley, for her generous financial contribution to the expenses of this project; to our critique team who gave such helpful feedback on the rough draft (Patricia Allan, Michael Babb, Darlene Bogle, Pam Davies, Carol Fryer, Cathy Haas, Ross Hayduk, Dorothy Holmes, Doug Houck, Dave Johnson, Kristy Keith, Dawn Killion, Alan Medinger, Kevin Oshiro, John Paulk, Janine Puls, Brad Sargent, Pat Smith, Jay Stone, Renee Tryon); to many ex-gay ministry leaders who have contributed so much to our understanding of homosexual recovery, especially to those who graciously permitted us to quote from their writings and lectures; to all the former homosexuals who bravely shared with us the intimate details of their lives in order to provide anecdotes for this book; to our friends and coworkers in ministries around the world who believed in this project and who prayed for its successful completion.

1

CAN HOMOSEXUALS REALLY CHANGE?

*F*rom childhood Mike Reed felt different *from other boys.* "Hey, sissy!" they would taunt him on the school playground. "You throw that ball like a girl!" Sometimes the attacks went further than words, like the time some boys put needles in their shoes with the points sticking out from the inside. Then they cornered Mike on the playing field and kicked him hard enough to draw blood. After that he started shaking whenever any of the "tough" boys approached him.

In high school Mike landed a part in the school play and began hanging out with the kids in theater. He discovered many of them had also experienced peer rejection, so they banded together for mutual support. But he did not tell even his closest friends about his growing sexual attraction to other men.

When Mike had his first homosexual encounter while in college, he felt like he had finally found himself. After that initial experience, he began to frequent gay bars and became involved in numerous sexual relationships with other men.

Then Mike "fell in love" with a man and they began a long-term relationship. *This is what I've always been looking for,* Mike told himself. He felt as if his needs for male love and attention were finally being met.

But the "long-term" relationship only lasted a year and then fell apart. Mike began a spiritual search which led him through mysti cism, yoga, Religious Science, Christian Science and finally to Christ.

"Two friends from work took me to a church where I heard that Jesus died for my sins," Mike recalls. "After that I started pulling away from the gay bars."

Then Mike saw an attractive man at church whom he had previous- ly seen in the bars. They talked after the service and felt an instant bond. *We're both gay and we also have a common faith in God,* Mike thought. It seemed like the perfect basis for a relationship and soon they were sexually involved.

Two weeks later both of them became convicted that something was wrong. One night in bed, Mike's lover turned to him and said, "We can't do this anymore. It's wrong." He opened his Bible and showed Mike where it forbade homosexual relationships.

"The Scriptures hit me like a brick between the eyes," Mike admits. "We got down on our knees and asked the Lord to help us turn away from homosexuality."

Mike moved into a home with two other Christian friends who had no past gay experiences, and his spiritual journey began in earnest. Even when he worked in a restaurant about two blocks from one of the gay bars and his old friends came in and harassed him, Mike stood firm. He began to see the dissatisfaction and emptiness in their eyes that previously he had felt in his own heart.

Eventually, Mike heard about Love In Action, a Christian ministry located in San Rafael, California, which specialized in helping people overcome homosexuality. He joined their live-in program in June 1979. During the months that followed, Mike began to deal with deep issues in his life, such as his masculine identity, feelings of inferiority to other men, discipline of his thought life, and the need to form healthy friendships with other straight men in his church.[1]

Slowly over the next several years Mike began to experience sig- nificant and lasting changes. His friendships with other men especial- ly transformed his life, as God used them to minister healing and acceptance. At times he was discouraged by continuing homosexual temptations, but he persisted in seeking change.

"As I persevered, God brought me through," Mike says. He read in the Bible over and over how much God loved him and had a purpose for his life. "A renewing of my mind was taking place, but it took time. I had to be patient."

As he gained confidence, Mike slowly began taking more of a leadership role in the worship team at his church. Eventually, he led worship regularly for the congregation of two hundred adults. Although he still struggled at times with memories of his past involvement in homosexuality, Mike pushed forward into new challenges and friendships. He wanted everything that God had planned for his life.

Then Mike began dating women he met at his church. One of these relationships matured into a serious commitment, and in 1987 Mike was married. Today he and his wife, Helen, have three children.

Now Mike says his previous lifestyle seems far behind him. "I see myself as a fulfilled man, as a strong and stable person. I don't look at myself as being homosexual. I don't even think of myself as 'ex-gay' so much. It's an area that I relate to less and less."

Change Is Possible
Mike Reed is just one of hundreds of men we know personally who have overcome homosexuality. We are also familiar with numerous women who have experienced similar changes in overcoming a lesbian past.

Starla Allen is one example. "My childhood was normal in many ways," she recalls. "Though my parents were strict, I knew they loved each other. Our home was secure. Yet, looking back, I'm aware of several events that helped set me up to later pursue a lesbian relationship."

When Starla was four years old, her family visited her grandparents. "Amid all the chit-chat, my grandfather started teasing me and he hurt my feelings. I started crying. My father didn't know how to respond. He took me into a bedroom and told me to stay there until I could 'pull myself together.' I felt ashamed, like I was being punished. *I won't show that kind of emotion again to Dad,* I promised myself.

"As my younger sister and I grew up, our parents warned us about the dangers of men, especially strangers," Starla remembers. "My father once told me, 'If anyone ever hurts my little girl, I'll kill him.' "

One night when Starla was thirteen, she'd been babysitting for a couple she knew. As the man drove her home afterward, anxious thoughts went through Starla's mind: *Why is he stopping at the liquor store on the way to my house? And why is he turning onto this dirt road?* The man parked the car right next to a lake, with Starla's door opening directly over the water. "Why are you doing this?" Starla yelled, as this man pinned her down against the seat of the car. Panicking, she realized there was no way to escape without further bodily harm. He proceeded to rape her.

"I remember the awful feeling of being violated, of having my own emotions totally ignored while he fulfilled his desires. I wondered if I'd done anything to encourage his advances. I didn't think so. Still, I felt deeply ashamed."

After the rape, Starla also remembered her dad's warnings about men. "I honestly feared Dad might kill this guy if I told him what had happened. If Dad did that, he could go to jail. I decided to tell no one, just stuff the whole experience down inside myself and forget about it."

Outwardly, Starla's parents noticed that she started acting a little tougher and "more ornery." She dressed in baggy shirts and blue jeans, wore no makeup, and kept her hair cut short. But they attributed all this to normal teenage behavior.

Throughout high school, Starla tried dating. But a deep-seated fear and hatred of men had already taken root in her heart. "Unconsciously, I viewed men as adversaries to be conquered. With that attitude, my dating life was a disaster, which proved not only that I didn't need men, but that they didn't need me, either."

In college, Starla met Kathy, who seemed to be a kindred spirit. "I taught her how to fence. She taught me to play handball. But what really affected me was her offer to pay for our sodas after a handball game. I knew she was very short on money, yet she offered to do this. Such a little thing, yet it made me feel like I could let down my guard with her. As I began to open up, we developed a deep emotional connection. I even shared my rape experience with her. Gradually, a physical attraction developed between us and we became lovers.

"We were together for about five years. The first few years were full of romance. But eventually, I realized I was sacrificing myself to this relationship, much more than she was. I did the housecleaning, shopping and cooking so she could pursue her artistic talent. Eventually, she started seeing a man. When I objected to this, she snapped, 'You can either learn to handle it, or we're through.' "

Starla stayed with her lover, though the relationship continued to crumble. In desperation, she also tried dating a young man she knew. But her emotional pain continued to build to the point where suicide seemed like a reasonable option.

"I even had my method of suicide picked out. In my emptiness, I surveyed the wreckage of my life. Was this all there was? Then I remembered the words of Mom Nelson, a woman who'd headed a girls' group back in high school. 'Jesus can really change your life,' she always said. I thought, *Well, I've tried everything else. I might as well give him a chance.*" Starla uttered a simple prayer: "God, if you're up there, I'm giving you three days. Here is my life. See what you can do."

Exactly three days later, Starla ran into Mrs. Nelson and told her about the prayer. They found a quiet spot nearby and had a long talk. Then they prayed together, and Starla asked God to forgive her past and help her begin again.

Starla moved to her own apartment and spent hours alone reading the Bible. She found a local church where she felt much love and acceptance, even after she shared her past with some of the church members. "My first year as a Christian was like a honeymoon period. Sexual temptation was not a big problem. I felt I'd finally found Someone who would give me all the love I could stand."

Over the years, Starla's healing has come in many ways. "The most significant change I've experienced is in being released from my hatred of men," she says. "First, I reached a point where I knew God just wanted me to be *willing* to forgive men, including the man who raped me. He knew I could not forgive emotionally, but he just wanted my willingness. The best I could do was to pray, 'OK, God, I'll try.' This hatred of men was such a stronghold, but over time, with prayer and even fasting, I could feel my attitudes changing. Eventually, I reached the point where I could actually pray for the man who raped me and mean it."

Today, Starla is a Ph.D. candidate. As a therapist, she helps both men and women find healing and resolution from damaged emotions. But her experience especially equips her to offer encouragement to other women seeking to come out of a lesbian past.

"Close, caring relationships with other godly men and women have been so important," she says. "The freedom to talk and share my emotions with others has helped remove the blanket of guilt and blame under which I suffocated for so many years. As I've realized I in no way encouraged the man who raped me, I no longer need to hide the woman within me. I am free to dress, feel, think and respond in ways that express my femininity. I'm discovering the woman who was suppressed inside of me for so long."[2]

For the man or woman struggling with homosexuality, there is hope for healing and new freedom in Christ!

The authors of this book, Bob Davies and Lori Rentzel, have worked in the field of ex-gay ministry since 1979, when we both joined the staff of Love In Action in San Rafael, California. Both of us have been involved in the leadership of Exodus International, a worldwide referral and resource network of ex-gay ministries; since 1985, Bob has served as executive director for Exodus. Despite similarities in our ministry involvement, however, we entered this field of ministry for very different reasons.

Lori's Story

One October evening in 1977, I settled in to work my shift as a phone counselor for a twenty-four-hour Christian crisis hotline in Minneapolis. While I stared at the phones, waiting for the lines to start buzzing, a friend of mine placed a copy of the Love In Action newsletter in my hands. "Lori, look at this."

I read that Love In Action was looking for someone with writing skills, office background, and an interest in homosexuality to work in their ministry office and put together counseling materials.

"That sounds like me," I said, and my friend agreed. In addition to phone counseling at the hotline, I had studied journalism in college, worked a few years as a newspaper reporter, and was currently a receptionist. More significantly, I had recently learned a lot about homosexuality, more than I had ever expected to know. Through a relationship with a close friend who was seeking Christian help in overcoming homosexuality, I had discovered that such help was hard to come by. For people getting out of drugs, alcohol, or even prostitution, Christian counseling and support were plentiful. For the man or woman trying to break out of homosexuality such counseling was almost nonexistent.

Also, back in 1977, material on homosexuality written from a Christian perspective was scarce. A few balanced articles were available, but most tended to be poorly written, discouraging or sensationalistic. ("I was delivered of ten demons of homosexuality, and now I'm totally free!")

After reading the Love In Action newsletter, I was excited by the opportunity to be personally involved in changing this bleak situation. An exchange of letters and a visit to the ministry confirmed to all involved that I belonged at Love In Action, so in January 1979, I boarded a Northwest Orient jet, leaving icebound Minneapolis for the lush, green hills of San Rafael, California.

I passionately believed the Bible promised healing and change for people coming out of homosexuality and lesbianism. My goal, when I arrived at Love In Action, was to communicate this hope through writing. But nothing worthwhile comes easily. Being involved in ministry to men and women changing something as deep as sexual identity exacts a price. I didn't remain a detached, helpful observer for long. In the process of equipping me to minister to others, God allowed me to face my own desperate inner sins, struggles, misbeliefs and insecurities.

For the next few years, I lived in the ministry's community houses, sharing daily life with both men and women coming out of the gay and lesbian lifestyles. We spent countless hours talking, praying, crying, sharing confidences—plus just hanging out and having fun together. Some of my deepest and best relationships were formed in those years.

In sharing homes and friendships with women seeking healing from lesbianism, I learned a lot about myself. Areas of shakiness in my own sexual identity quickly surfaced. Though I have never been involved in a lesbian relationship, I did go through a period of several months during which I experienced strong sexual and emotional attractions to women. I had to examine hurts and attitudes within myself and get counsel and prayer support from trusted Christian men and women around me.

Those particular temptations passed, but never again will I view my sexuality as something set in stone. And not a year goes by where I do not question, examine and pray about some facet of what it means to be a woman or uncover some new area of my sexuality that needs healing or redefining. As the mother of three small daughters, I have added motivation for discovering and embracing God's full intent for me as a woman.

Bob and I have done much reading and research on homosexuality and lesbianism, examining both from secular *and* Christian viewpoints. Both of us have experienced much healing in our lives and sexuality. But perhaps the best thing we have to share in this book is our experience of living for years "in the trenches" with men and women going through the excruciating, amazing process of being healed in their sexual identities. We've been there, talking through decisions, grappling with hard questions, seeing hope come into people's faces. We've struggled alongside, sharing in the journey of healing.

We are well-acquainted with how tough this journey is, too well-acquainted to sit in harsh judgment on friends and counselees who have opted to return to homosexual involvement. Yet we have witnessed solid, substantial healing in so many men and women over so many years that we can say without hesitation, "There is a way out of homosexuality. For the man or woman who truly desires it, there is hope and healing in Christ."

Bob's Story

I will never forget the day when, at age fourteen, I read a book for teens on the "facts of life." Near the end was a chapter that described the symptoms of homosexuality. Much to my horror, I discovered that every single quality applied to me!

I had been raised in the church; prayer, daily Bible reading and weekly Sunday School attendance were ingrained habits. *So how could I have this problem?* I wondered.

Rather than seek help, I hid my fears, withdrew from everyone and eventually quit going to church. Why bother, when God seemed irrelevant to my deepest needs?

In my late teens, while a freshman at the University of British Columbia in Vancouver, Canada, I checked out books on homosexuality and learned of the large gay subculture in many North American cities. Curious, I began visiting adult bookstores and reading homosexual magazines. Only guilt and fear kept me from pursuing actual sexual encounters with other men.

Eventually, several years later, I made a renewed commitment to my childhood faith and was accepted as a student at Prairie Bible College in Three Hills, Alberta. During the next three years, I was spiritually strengthened by a constant diet of God's Word, both in the classroom and my private studies. My self-confidence blossomed as I experienced close friendships with other men—something I had never known before. Yet I kept my homosexual desires a deeply hidden secret.

Two years after graduation, I attended a discipleship training school in Germany run by Youth With A Mission, a worldwide evangelistic ministry. After the six-month program, I began praying about my future. How did God want me to serve him?

One morning during prayer, I saw myself back home, handing out tracts in front of Vancouver's largest gay bar. My heart sank. *No way,* I moaned inwardly. *I'll do* anything—*except that!*

Over the next several years I tried to forget about my continuing homosexual struggles. I started training for the mission field. I was still sexually abstinent, but the pull toward homosexual relationships was growing stronger. Then one day I read a book which mentioned Love In Action, and I requested their monthly newsletter. Finally, in 1978, I came to the realization that my sexual struggles would never be resolved without some specialized help. I wrote Love In Action (LIA) and asked for an application to their live-in program. I arrived on their doorstep June 1, 1979.

That summer I made some startling discoveries. I realized that, because of my own sexual struggles, I could give meaningful support to others facing similar battles. And because I had never fallen into homosexual behavior, I could offer valuable insights on perseverance and spiritual warfare.

My initial summer's commitment grew to six months, then one year. Before long I realized my life had taken a permanent turn. I began editing the ministry's monthly newsletter, writing new literature and speaking at local seminars.

God continued to work in my own life. Much to my surprise, I discovered that homosexuality was *not* my sole problem. The illicit same-sex desires were only an outward symptom of deeper emotional wounds that needed healing. Through LIA's support group, I was able to openly confess such struggles as insecurity, fear and envy of other men.

The unconditional love of my church was also crucial to my growth—especially support from straight men. Because of my position on staff with Love In Action everyone knew of my past. But the men at my church were not afraid to show their acceptance by a smile or warm hug.

All my life I had struggled with feelings of inferiority around other men. But through affirmation from these Christian men, I slowly began to feel more like "one of the guys." I had received some of this same-sex affirmation at Bible college, and now the healing was continuing.

Then came the biggest shock of all. In 1984 I sensed that God was leading me into a marriage relationship. I sought confirmation and counsel from my pastor and closest friends. Nine months later, I was exchanging wedding vows with a pretty, brown-eyed brunette. A new adventure was about to begin!

Yet, even in marriage, my healing process continued. As a married man, I have grown in my role as husband, lover and friend to my wife, Pam. Like many men who have dealt with homosexuality, I struggle at times with passivity. I still hate confrontation, so God gives me plenty of opportunities to grow in that area (whether that means asking a macho neighbor in an upstairs apartment to turn down his blaring TV at 11:00 p.m., or telling my wife what I *really* think about her ideas for our vacation!).

Whether it's facing the roots of my homosexuality or some other challenge in my spiritual walk, I know that my growth will continue for a lifetime. And that is the same challenge and promise that every Christian faces. None of us has "arrived." We're all in this together!

What We've Learned

During the past fourteen years, we have become personally acquainted with hundreds of men and women who have left behind the gay and lesbian lifestyle. We will be sharing more of their experiences in coming chapters.

Through our combined years of practical ministry involvement, we have learned that each person seeking to overcome homosexuality is different. Those who have exited from homosexuality span a wide variety of ages, personalities, occupations and church denominations.

Some ex-gays and former lesbians were once immersed in the homosexual subculture of cities like San Francisco or New York for several decades. Others endured a silent struggle, confiding in no one, never having a homosexual experience—but wrestling deeply with same-sex fantasies and desires.

Now some of these men and women have been free from homosexual involvement for ten or twenty years. They are not just suppressing their strong homosexual or lesbian longings. There has been a true resolution of this issue in their lives.

There is no identical plan of action for healing, no quick fix or one-two-three formula. Some of these overcomers have found all the help they needed through their local church. Many others have found support through a local ex-gay ministry, like Love In Action, which offered counseling and weekly fellowship support groups. Still other men and women—those with deeply rooted symptoms needing professional expertise—have sought additional private psychological therapy.

This book may not answer all your questions. But we hope it will serve as an introduction to the most important issues that you will face as *you* seek to overcome homosexuality. As you read of how God worked in the lives of other men and women, you will gain insights and encouragement for your own recovery process.

2

BIBLICAL AND SCIENTIFIC EVIDENCE FOR CHANGE

*O*nce gay, always gay" is a common sentiment in the homosexual community. Many gays and lesbians feel that they were born homosexual. They do not remember making a conscious choice to be sexually drawn to members of their own sex. So, the common logic says, homosexuality must be genetic or hormonal, and there is nothing that can be done about it.

Such thinking seems logical, but we do not believe it is based in truth. Both the Scriptures and much secular literature provide evidence that homosexuality, though deeply ingrained and habitually practiced, can be overcome—both as a lifestyle and as an identity.

Looking for Truth
What does the Bible *really* say about homosexuality? Is *all* homosexual behavior forbidden? Or just promiscuous relationships without love or commitment?

I (Bob) have faced this question about the biblical perspective on homosexuality. As an eighteen-year-old college freshman, I discovered an impressive array of books on homosexuality at the university library. Some of these books presented the subject of homosexuality from a "religious" point of view, although all of them were favorable toward adopting homosexual practice as a normal lifestyle.

One Saturday morning I was lying in bed reading one of these theological treatises on homosexuality. As I read page after page of arguments justifying same-sex practices, my mind wanted so much to believe the words I was reading. *If only I could really embrace this viewpoint,* I thought, *all of the conflict I feel inside would be resolved.*

But, as hard as I tried to block it out, a stronger conviction refused to budge from my conscience: *This book is wrong. These arguments are wrong. Homosexuality is wrong!*

Tears of frustration came to my eyes as I realized that, no matter how much time I spent reading why homosexuality was an acceptable option for the Christian, I would never be able to believe it. I knew too much about the biblical stand on sex outside of marriage. Whether sex occurred between an unmarried man and woman or between two same-sex partners, the activity would always be fornication or adultery. No amount of justification or argument would change God's standard.

So I had a clear choice to make: Would I obey God's Word, or seek to reinterpret it in order to fulfill my sexual desires?

TIME OUT

Few former lesbians or ex-gay men embrace the Bible's position on homosexuality without some struggle. If you still feel an internal conflict over this issue, don't run from the struggle. Face it squarely, and spend some time sorting through the issues. We have prepared some answers to common pro-gay interpretations of Scriptures on homosexuality in appendix A. Perhaps you will want to take a break right now to look over that material before reading further in this chapter.

The Bible and Homosexuality

The Bible condemns homosexual practices in several places: Genesis

19:1-20; Leviticus 18:22; 20:13; Judges 19:1-25; Romans 1:24-27; 1 Corinthians 6:9-11; and 1 Timothy 1:9-11. The Romans passage includes a specific prohibition of both male and female homosexual involvement.[1] The Bible makes no positive statements about homosexuality. The only two options affirmed for adult Christians are heterosexual marriage or abstinence.

The vast majority of academic and biblical scholars agree that the Bible prohibits homosexual activities. Nearly all of today's credible translations of the Bible are also in agreement: homosexual practice is prohibited by God.

Furthermore, there is clear biblical evidence that God can change the life of a person involved in this behavior. In 1 Corinthians chapter six the apostle Paul is addressing men and women in the church at Corinth. He lists many forms of behavior—including homosexual involvement—that will bar someone from God's kingdom (v. 9). Then Paul makes an amazing statement: "And this is what some of you *were*. But you were washed, you were sanctified, you were justified in the name of the Lord Jesus Christ and by the Spirit of our God" (v. 11, emphasis added).

Paul knew former homosexuals in the church at Corinth! So the message that homosexuality can be changed is not new; homosexuals have been experiencing change since the Bible was written.

The church has prohibited homosexual relations since its inception. This stand is found not only in the biblical passages but also in other church writings from the earliest centuries after Christ. For example, *The Teaching of the Twelve Apostles,* written between A.D. 100 and 150, is an instruction manual for Christians. Some of the practices to be avoided: "You shall not commit murder, you shall not commit adultery, you shall not commit homosexual acts, you shall not steal."[2]

We could easily spend the rest of this book exploring the theology of homosexuality, but that is not our purpose. In the remainder of this book we will assume that you want to overcome homosexuality and that you are looking for specific, practical help in finding freedom.

Scientific Evidence

Other support for ex-gay ministry comes, surprisingly enough, from world-renowned researchers whose studies support the idea that homosexuality can be changed. Of course, there is great debate today among researchers as to the causes of homosexuality and the role that genetics and other prebirth factors might play.

√*No studies prove conclusively that homosexuality is inborn.* If such proof existed, it would be given instant worldwide publicity and the ongoing arguments would end. Despite the lack of conclusive evidence, many people believe that homosexuality is inborn. It certainly gives a ready explanation for why so many lesbians and homosexuals have always felt *different.* It could also explain why homosexual feelings and identity are difficult to change.

Periodically a scientific report on this subject is published that receives a great deal of media attention. For example, in the August 1991 issue of *Science,* researcher Simon LeVay published his study on the differences in brain structure between homosexual and heterosexual men.[3]

Newspapers and magazines across the country hailed the study as additional proof that homosexuality is inborn. LeVay's study was interesting, but we don't believe it offered any conclusive proof of genetic causes for homosexuality.

The study had several glaring weaknesses. First, it was based on a small group of thirty-five men. Second, the nineteen homosexual men in the study had died of AIDS, a factor which could have biased the results. Third, the control group of sixteen men were "assumed to have been mostly or all heterosexual."[4] This was quite an assumption for such an important study. Finally, cause and effect were not established. Did the men in the study become homosexual because of their brain structure, or did their brain structure change in response to their involvement in homosexuality? Many studies have found that brain cells change in response to a person's life experiences.[5] In summary, this research project had so many potential problems that one professor concluded, "My freshman biology students know enough to sink this study."[6]

The Bailey-Pillard study on twins was also widely reported in the media. Psychologist Michael Bailey of Northwestern University and psychiatrist Richard Pillard of the Boston University School of Medicine showed that if one identical twin is gay, the other is more than twice as likely to be gay than if the twins are fraternal. (Identical twins are the same genetically; but fraternal twins develop from two separate eggs fertilized by separate sperm, so they are genetically dissimilar.)[7]

This study is interesting but inconclusive. If homosexuality is purely genetic, identical twins should share the same sexual orientation, whether homosexual or heterosexual, one hundred percent of the time. When both twins are raised in the same household, the environmental impact on each twin cannot be factored out of the results. A better study to show the effect of genetics would observe the incidence of concurrent homosexuality in identical twins raised together in the same household versus the incidence in identical twins raised apart.[8]

Another Scientific Viewpoint

So these studies raise interesting questions, but none provides any solid evidence of inborn homosexuality. On the other hand, many psychological experts believe that homosexuality is *not* inborn and can be changed. The popular media rarely mention study results like these.

"I have recently had occasion to review the result of psychotherapy with homosexuals, and been surprised by the findings," said Dr. Reuben Fine, director for the New York Center for Psychoanalytic Training. "If the patients were motivated, whatever procedure is adopted, a large percentage will give up their homosexuality. In this connection, public information is of the greatest importance. The misinformation spread by certain circles that 'homosexuality is untreatable by psychotherapy' does incalculable harm to thousands of men and women."[9]

Sex researchers Masters and Johnson reported in their book *Homosexuality in Perspective* that the success rate in eighty-one gays desiring reorientation (after a six-year follow up), was 71.6 percent.[10] Their conclusion: "No longer should the qualified psychotherapist avoid the responsibility of either accepting the homosexual client in treatment or referring him or her to an acceptable treatment source."[11]

"The major challenge in treating homosexuality from the point of view of the patient's resistance has, of course, been the misconception that the disorder is innate or inborn," wrote Dr. Charles Socarides, attending psychiatrist and professor at the Albert Einstein College of Medicine in New York City, in the *American Handbook of Psychiatry.*[12]

Dr. Irving Bieber served as president of the New York Medical College and directed a research team in a nine-year study of male homosexuality. Here is what Bieber and his colleagues concluded: "The therapeutic results of our study provide reason for an optimistic outlook. Many homosexuals became exclusively heterosexual in psychoanalytic treatment. Although this change may be more easily accomplished by some than others, in our judgment, *a heterosexual shift is a possibility for all homosexuals who are strongly motivated to change*" (emphasis added).[13]

Seventeen years later Dr. Bieber stated, "We have followed some patients for as long as ten years who have remained exclusively heterosexual. Reversal estimates now range from 30% to an optimistic 50%."[14]

These debates are long and complex and will probably continue for many years. It would be beyond the scope of this book to go into great scientific detail. Ultimately, we believe that further studies will confirm what we already know, that healing is possible for homosexuals who are motivated to change.

How Long Does It Take?

The pace at which you experience change in your sexuality depends on several factors.

☐ *Your commitment to Christ and to the change process.* If you have made a solid decision to follow Christ and you welcome his work in every area of life, including your sexuality, you are off to a great start. The factors below will come into play as you seek healing, but the depth of your commitment to Christ will strongly correspond to the depth of your healing.

☐ *Your past homosexual or lesbian involvement.* You may have been deeply involved in homosexual or lesbian relationships for years, if not decades. Or you may have only thought of becoming involved. Some men remember being drawn to other boys since early childhood. Some women never had a lesbian thought or desire until twenty years after being married.

Our past sexual experiences are all recorded in the brain. They are not magically erased the moment we ask for God's forgiveness. Only a brain transplant would wipe them away—not a likely prospect! A significant part of the struggle in coming out of homosexuality is dealing with the memories and emotions linked to our past sinful actions.

☐ *Your reasons for becoming involved homosexually in the first place.*
Our motives for seeking sexual involvement differ widely. The underlying issues that give rise to homosexual desires can be completely
different from one person to the next. For example, some women enter
lesbianism after years of sexual abuse or other trauma at the hands
of fathers or other older males. Their underlying fears and motivations for seeking affection from other women can be deeply rooted and
complex.

Other women grow up in a healthy family environment, but
through disillusioning experiences with the opposite sex or the influence of the feminist movement they become involved in a lesbian
relationship. Their recovery process may occur at a faster rate.

Similarly, some men have deep emotional wounds going back to
their early childhood which have to be faced and healed. Others became confused in their sexual identity after being sexually molested
by another male, although they had previously been moving toward
heterosexual relationships. Each person's situation is different; therefore each person's pathway to overcoming homosexuality will also be
unique.

☐ *Your participation in the process of change.* For a season, some
former homosexuals choose to devote a major portion of their time and
energy to their recovery process. For example, one former lesbian
joined a support group for recovering homosexuals, then spent many
hours each day poring over the handouts and her Bible, entering
insights into her journal and praying with her new friends in the
group. Three years after her last lesbian relationship, she was happily
married and feeling secure in her new identity.

☐ *God's sovereignty.* One factor in your recovery process is not under
your control. For reasons we cannot explain, God chooses to work
more quickly in some lives than in others.

One married man was deeply involved in promiscuous homosexual
activities, then he became a Christian. Literally overnight his homosexual temptations disappeared, and his heterosexual marriage relationship was restored. (This is a very unusual situation.)

Other men and women submit their sexuality to God for his healing, then walk in faithful obedience to his Word. They experience
change, but at a much slower rate. Regardless of the pace of change
or the time period involved, genuine change is worth the effort.

Will I Become Heterosexual?

The goal of the ex-gay or former lesbian is wholeness in *all* areas of life, including the capacity for healthy, close relationships with the opposite sex. This dynamic of life is true for everyone, male and female, whether they are single or married.

Many former homosexuals eventually go on to experience marriage and parenthood. This option is certainly possible, but it should not be your initial goal in seeking recovery. We have found that some ex-gays make the mistake of idealizing marriage, as if it will solve all their problems. Your married friends can give you a "reality check" on that fantasy!

Of course, being married does not prove that a former homosexual is "healed." We have talked to many people who are married and still struggling with homosexual feelings and behavior. They live with each foot in a different world, feeling trapped in a heterosexual façade while secretly longing for same-gender sexual intimacy. They are usually desperately unhappy. (If you are in this situation, chapter thirteen is written just for you.) A wedding ring does not mean that your homosexual issues are resolved.

But back to the question. We need to clarify one thing. What do we mean by the word *heterosexual?*

Many people strive for our cultural norm, rather than seeking the level of sexual purity to which God calls us. For example, you may wonder if you will ever experience a strong, even passionate, lust when looking at an attractive member of the opposite sex on the beach. It's possible, but this certainly is not our goal in being healed. God does not replace one form of lust with another.

Rather than opposite-sex lust, healing for both women and men means experiencing sexual interest in the opposite sex, as well as having healthy friendships with both men and women. To us this constitutes true, godly heterosexuality.

If you experience resolution of your homosexuality and God eventually leads you into marriage, certainly you can expect to have a fulfilling sexual relationship with your spouse. Sexual experiences in marriage can be just as exciting for the former homosexual as for anybody else.

Recovery Is a Process

Spiritual growth is a lifelong process. Working through character faults and past hurts, immaturities and insecurities is a long process for *everyone,* not just the recovering homosexual or lesbian.

Some ex-gay men and women get so focused on the issue of homosexuality that they forget other Christians have a "past" too. In many ways you are not all that different from other believers. Resist the tendency to look at others in your church as better than yourself. "They look like they have it all together," you sigh. "Look, all the people my age are already married and have kids. I'm such a failure!"

One ex-gay man, Griffin, was feeling insecure about his own progress until he went to a men's weekend retreat and got better acquainted with some of the guys in his church. After one evening message on sexual purity, many of the men confessed their struggles with habitual masturbation, pornography and impure thoughts. One married man said he was coming out of a season of being strongly tempted to commit adultery with a woman he had met at work. Another older man shared his story of being abused as a youth and his subsequent sexual confusion.

Griffin realized that his own struggles with self-image and lust as a former homosexual were not so unusual after all. Most straight men, he discovered, fought similar battles.

Our ultimate goal is to become like Jesus Christ—whole and complete in every aspect of our being. Homosexuality is just one manifestation of our brokenness and incompleteness. As we grow into God's image, we will increasingly become the person he created us to be in *all* areas of life.

3

THE DYNAMICS OF CHANGE

*O*ur deliverance from homosexuality comes from a Person, rather than a method," says Frank Worthen, who spent more than twenty years in homosexuality before leaving that lifestyle and starting Love In Action in 1973.

As Frank discovered, the interesting thing about the change process is that change itself is not our goal. Change is what *results* as we pursue a far more important and compelling goal: knowing, loving and "beholding" Jesus.

"And we, who with unveiled faces all reflect the Lord's glory, are being transformed into his likeness with ever-increasing glory, which comes from the Lord, who is the Spirit" (2 Cor 3:18).

In coming out of homosexuality, we sometimes focus *too* intensely on our inner hang-ups, misbeliefs, past hurts and sinful tendencies. Looking inward, we may feel as if we're gazing into an ever-deepening pool of confusion and despair.

Release and healing come as we look upward—to Jesus—and enter more deeply into fellowship with him. The cry of our heart becomes, *God, I want to know you. I want to love and worship you. I want to be a man or woman who reflects your image. Cleanse me from everything that stands between you and me.*

God delights to answer such a prayer. He alone understands the complex combination of choices and circumstances that have shaped us to make us who we are today. He is fully aware of our pain and our weaknesses, yet his vision of "who we are in Christ" far exceeds our powers of imagination. His desire for us surpasses—and, in fact, inspires—our desire for him.

Change is a cooperative venture between God and ourselves through the power of the Holy Spirit. His grace woos and empowers us to make the choices that lead to freedom in our sexuality and in every other area of life. We seek him and he reveals to us not only who he is but who we are as well.

Some of us struggle with a distorted view of God that makes it difficult for us to trust him, especially in such sensitive areas as sexuality and identity. We may not be able to separate our image of God from that of an abusive or disappointing authority figure in our past. When this is true, we can confess this to God and ask him to heal us of this misperception. He is faithful to do this in ways that personally speak to us and reassure us.

Surrender and Change

Why do some people make it out of homosexuality while others don't? We have thought a lot about this question, reflecting on the many people we know who have made a firm and lasting break from homosexuality and on others who have not.

One common denominator among those men and women experiencing significant change involves the issue of *control* in their lives. These individuals have decided to follow Christ and do his will at any cost.

Perhaps you have heard sermons about "surrendering" or "yielding" to Christ and wonder what this implies about your struggles. Some feel revolted at the whole idea of surrender, fearing they will lose their autonomy to the control of a celestial dictator. Others welcome the thought, hoping to be released from the constant challenge of making difficult choices and decisions.

Basically, surrender is an act of faith. It is a step of deep commitment, which involves: (1) giving God permission to work in our life as he pleases, and (2) making a decision to trust him in the midst of our life circumstances, believing he is working through them for our ultimate good.

When I (Lori) first accepted Christ in 1973, my commitment was at best reluctant. Mentally I was convinced that Christianity was true, that "Jesus was the Way." But I remember attending a prayer meeting where everyone was singing "The cross before me, the world behind me . . ." Looking around at this circle of believers, their eyes closed in reverent worship, I wanted to run out of the room. The cross did seem to loom before me. But the world sure wasn't behind me. In fact, it looked pretty good to me that night.

For the next year and a half I was miserable. Every day was a battle just to remain interested in God. I felt more at home at a keg party than at a Bible study, yet I felt like a hypocrite in both places. I knew too much of God to deny his reality, but my efforts to peacefully coexist with him were producing unbearable strain and tension.

Finally I was able to see that *having Christ in my life* was not going to work. What God actually was requiring of me was that I *have my life in Christ* (Rom 6:11).

Author C. S. Lewis said, "Fallen man is not simply an imperfect creature who needs improvement: he is a rebel who must lay down his arms."[1] I made a decision to come to God on his terms—unconditional surrender. *God, I want your way,* I prayed. *I want Jesus to be Lord of my life.* And I meant it.

The relief that came over me was exhilarating. While I still encountered difficult challenges and painful choices, the Christian life became a joy and a strength to me rather than a burden to be endured. God and I were on the same team now, facing the battle together. He was my rock, my ally, rather than my enemy.

All Christians face the decision of accepting or rejecting Christ's lordship. However, the former homosexual faces it sooner than most.

Coming out of homosexuality into wholeness requires deep emotional healing and a restructuring of our whole identity. As our Creator, God is the only one who knows exactly how to restore our personality. For him to complete this healing work he calls for our cooperation.

Our natural tendencies are to squirm off the operating table, run when we should rest, and quit taking our antibiotics as soon as we feel better. The grace and power to resist these tendencies come as we get to know the Lord better, learning to trust in his care for us.

There are times when life's pressures seem intolerable and its rewards nonexistent. But these are the times when God remains faithful to the commitment we have made to him. In the midst of heartache and extreme difficulties, he shows us his infinite ability to resolve impossible situations.

The Choice to Surrender

For some former homosexuals, coming face-to-face with this decision of a deeper surrender to Christ can happen at unexpected times in unexpected ways.

At church one Sunday morning in September 1978, I (Bob) learned that a well-known evangelist would be speaking in the evening service. I spent the rest of the day reading his autobiography, which told stories of his adventures sharing Christ around the globe. That evening I went to church filled with expectation, ready to hear a challenging testimony.

Things didn't go as I had expected. During the service, I could sense the speaker's deep commitment to Jesus Christ. I heard about the thousands of lives he had impacted, and I felt convicted about my own shallow commitment.

Lord, I prayed, *I want my life to count like that man's life is counting for your kingdom.* In my spirit I sensed an unexpected question: *Are you willing to pay the price?*

I pondered that question for the next three days.

I sensed God challenging me to give him every part of my life in a much deeper way than I ever had before. I felt his spotlight shining on one dark area of my life—my homosexuality—that I had kept carefully hidden from everyone. For years, I had offered many prayers: *God, please take this problem away* and *Lord, if you will heal my homosexuality, I will be an on-fire Christian. Then my life will* really *count for your kingdom.*

None of my past prayers seemed to make much difference.

Now I knew God was calling me to a deeper commitment than anything I'd experienced, and I didn't like it. I wanted to hang on to ... what? My homosexuality? Not really. But there was something in the way, some unseen barrier preventing me from total surrender.

Perhaps it was pride. And fear? Yes, I was terrified of what God would ask. Maybe someday I would have to tell others about my homosexual struggles. My heart pounded at such a horrifying possibility.

Over the next several days I fought and kicked, firmly resisting God's challenge. Finally, exhausted, in the early hours of a late summer night, I yielded. *OK, God. I will give this area of my life to you.* This simple statement marked a major turning point in my life.

My decision did not instantly release me from homosexuality; rather, it opened me up for God to begin working in a deeper way. Since that day in 1978 God has gradually overhauled my life, a transformation that has affected my career, my personality and my sexuality.

TIME OUT
Have you ever given God specific permission to work in *every* area of your life, including your sexuality? Take a few minutes to write down any fears you have about this decision. Yielding control of these areas to God will open you up for him to work in new ways in your life.

Submitting Our Homosexuality
Now let's look at specific applications of this principle to the issue of recovery from homosexuality and lesbianism.

□ *Surrendering to Christ means learning to obey him a step at a time in the process of recovery.* For some this step may mean opening up for the first time to another individual regarding their homosexuality.

Jim said, "I've prayed for years against these feelings, but nothing has worked." But Jim had never confessed his struggles to anyone except God. Like Jim, many people will not consider this option. They discount it as impossible because of their position in church, their prominence in a small community, or their fear of losing a job, a marriage, a family.

These are legitimate concerns, but all of us need the support and encouragement of others. There is power in mutual confession. "If we walk in the light, as he is in the light, we have fellowship with one another, and the blood of Jesus, his Son, purifies us from every sin" (1 Jn 1:7).

☐ *Acknowledging Christ's lordship means trusting in his timing for recovery.* The God-do-this-now-or-else mindset is a deadly pitfall in the healing process. Think about a doctor's response if a cancer patient said, "I'll give you two months to fix me. If your treatments don't eradicate every symptom of cancer, I'll quit." Similarly, we cannot put time limits on our healing process. God has a unique timetable for each of us.

☐ *Yielding to Christ means persevering despite painful emotions or powerful attractions.* We may experience intense rage, sorrow or jealousy, and yet be progressing wonderfully in our healing process. Sometimes God waits until we have developed a solid level of trust with him before allowing such emotions to surface. Likewise, we may find ourselves overwhelmed with feelings of homosexual or lesbian desire. These may come from any number of sources, including satanic attack and fatigue. Or they may be surfacing along with many other repressed feelings. When these emotions occur, we can acknowledge them, pray for God's strength to deal with them, then seek understanding and healing for the underlying issues.

Avenues of Change
Christians throughout the ages have had sinful habits to overcome and misbeliefs to replace with truth. The same Christian disciplines that have helped them will help you too.

☐ *Practicing God's presence.* A powerful discipline and channel of healing is learning to practice God's presence: quieting ourselves before God, resting in him, enjoying his fellowship. "Be still, and know that I am God" (Ps 46:10).

We can practice God's presence as we do our work, visit with a friend, take a shower or cut up vegetables for dinner. I (Lori) like to quiet myself before God to prepare for times of prayer and intercession. Sometimes I get so relaxed in God's presence that I never do get around to putting my prayers into words, yet I come away assured that my heart's petitions have been heard.

Another wonderful aspect of practicing God's presence is what author and lecturer Leanne Payne describes as "listening for the healing word." Her book, *The Broken Image,* is a great resource on the effectiveness of healing prayer in overcoming homosexuality and lesbianism.

On listening to God, she says: "Thus, in the Presence, listening to the word the Spirit sends, spiritual and psychological healing takes place. Our Lord sends a word—of joy, judgment, instruction, guidance. And that word, if hidden away in an obedient heart, will work toward the integration of that personality. As I listen and obey, I *become.*"[2]

As we listen to God, spending time in his presence, we discover our true identity in Christ.

☐ *Praying for ourselves.* In our personal prayer times, we need to be honest with God about our homosexual or lesbian thoughts, desires and struggles. He is not shocked by confessions of involvement in masturbation, pornography or other sexual sins. Nothing we do or say comes as a surprise to him. Confessing our sins and shortcomings to God is the only means to forgiveness (1 Jn 1:9), and each of us needs a clean start every day, free from the weight of condemnation from our past.

Most of us go through times when prayer feels like a dry habit. We can help alleviate this by being as specific as possible in our prayers, letting God know our deepest heart's desires, our hopes for how he will work in our lives. Many people record their prayers, leaving a blank space to write in the date when God answered that prayer and how. (Don't forget to go back in your list and record answers!)

Others have found encouragement from visual aids which remind that God answers prayer. Jane, for example, keeps a large jar near her bed. When God answers a specific prayer, she drops a colored marble into the jar. As the weeks have come and gone, Jane has been amazed at the number of marbles that now sit in her bedroom as a colorful reminder of God's interest in her life.

☐ *Praying for others.* We may be burdened for our old friends who are still actively involved in homosexuality. Sometimes they are not interested in hearing about our decision to seek change. Prayer is a powerful way of reaching out to them, whether they are aware of it or not.

Here are some specific ideas on praying for old friends. Write down the names of friends you think about who are still pursuing homosexuality. Ask God to open their eyes to the truth about where their sexual choices are leading. Pray that God will prolong the lives of your friends who have AIDS, and ask that he bring Christians into their lives who can love them and share the truths of eternity with them in a noncondemning way. *If you have just left the gay lifestyle, you are not strong enough to go back and witness to your friends. But you can be very effective in prayer.* Turn your concerns into prayer requests.

☐ *Praising and worshiping.* "The individuals most likely to leave homosexuality behind," says Frank Worthen, "are those who have an excitement about God, an anticipation of what he will do next in their lives. They see him at work even in small details, and their hearts are full of praise."

The psalms, particularly the songs of David, illustrate the powerful effect of releasing deep emotions to the Lord through music. Here is how music played a healing role in helping one woman come out of the lesbian lifestyle.

Deborah's childhood was marked by trauma, including repeated episodes of sexual abuse. She grew up "emotionally frozen," with little sense of boundaries or security. Even after becoming a Christian, Deborah stumbled from one sinful relationship to another. Then, after experiencing God's presence in a new way at a women's retreat, the Lord gave her a key to unlock her emotions: singing.

"God showed me that if I would sing out my hurts and feelings, they would come to the surface and be healed." One day while singing songs of praise, Deborah recalls, "God's praise broke into my heart as never before. I had a wonderful sense of being a newborn baby, cradled in her daddy's arms. I felt warm and secure, and looked up to see God's eyes of love for the very first time."

Later, Deborah raced across a field with outstretched arms, shouting and laughing in her newfound discovery of God the Father's love. "Daddy loves me! My daddy loves me!" she yelled over and over again, her heart bursting with joy. God had revealed himself to her in a new, direct and profound way.[3]

☐ *Studying the Bible.* Jack was an avid Bible reader, but he found that he had trouble remembering specific verses. Someone suggested he begin a "personal concordance." Jack bought a lined notebook, then began watching for special verses that applied to his struggles. These he wrote in his notebook under different headings. Jack struggled with homosexual fantasies, so he watched for verses he could write under his "Thought Life" heading. He also struggled with pornography, so he recorded such verses as "I will set before my eyes no vile thing" (Ps 101:3) in another section. Jack also adapted verses slightly to apply them directly to his situation: "I have made a covenant with my eyes not to look lustfully at a man" (Job 31:1). Jack found that there were *many* verses that did not specifically mention homosexuality but which were applicable to his everyday struggles.

Other possible headings for a personal concordance include the root issues of homosexuality and the emotions you are dealing with during this time in your life (feeling inferior, afraid of other Christians, loneliness, sexual frustration, masturbation, fear, healthy relationships, femininity, dealing with parents).

The main point here is to personalize the Scriptures to your own life and struggles. Although it is helpful to read and even memorize the Bible, the key is *application.* Biblical principles and insights must be worked into the fabric of your life before you will begin to see effective change.[4]

☐ *Journaling.* Recording our thoughts in a journal is an excellent way of tracking our forward progress. We all tend to feel that we are stagnating at times. If we can go back and read through old journals, we will immediately see our growth. "A journal is a good road map to see how far you've come," says Deborah, who has kept a journal since high school.

Journaling is different from keeping a diary. Instead of writing day-to-day events, in a journal you record your emotions and impressions of what God is doing in your life. Some people write in their journals daily, others weekly or several times a month. You can include poems and prayers to God, as well as spiritual goals for the next week, month or year. Several excellent Christian books are available on journal techniques.[5]

This activity is especially recommended for those of you who don't have someone right now to whom you can "spill your guts." Writing down your thoughts and prayers is an excellent method of self-therapy. "You will find depths of healing that you will not find in the presence of another person," says one former lesbian. "Journaling offers a tremendous opportunity for us to enter into intimacy with the Lord."

"You'll discover that as you write down your problems, many times you'll find the answers right in front of you," says Jeff Konrad, a former homosexual and author of *You Don't Have to Be Gay.* "I can't begin to tell you how many times I went to my journal and reread sections of it for encouragement. There were depressing days when I wasn't doing well and I was thinking, *What's the use, I've failed again.* But after reading parts of my journal, I could see just how far I'd come. A lot had changed; I had grown in many ways."[6]

A Christian Support Network

In examining the question of why some people make it out of homosexuality while others don't, we have noticed two interrelated characteristics common among those who are successful: (1) the extent of their separation from their gay support network, and (2) the quality of their involvement with a local church.

God has made us social creatures. Most people, even introverts, do not exist happily in complete isolation from others. We all desire to spend time with others who share our interests, whether it's through joining the local health club, attending AA meetings, supporting a certain political candidate, or joining a local drama or music group. Through group involvement, our social needs are met and our interests and skills are reinforced.

When you come away from homosexuality, there may be a huge vacuum left in your social life. Some other group of people must replace your gay social circles, or you will be drawn back in. Few, if any, people leave homosexuality on their own. Nearly all the ex-gays we know have made this difficult transition with the strong support of Christian friends. Most of these significant friendships have formed through local church involvement. *Unless your relationships with other Christians become (and remain) stronger than your relationships with gay friends, you will probably return to homosexual involvement.* That's a strong statement, but we have found it true in almost all of the ex-gays we've known over the years. The gay community doesn't want defectors. Neither does Christ. Whom do you desire to serve?

For you, as a Christian, the church is the natural place to find a new network of supportive friends for your healing journey. Homosexual behavior, like any sin, is overcome by God's power. God uses people in this process, and he has established the local church as a place for healing and interpersonal support. In Hebrews 10:25 this principle is clearly stated: "Let us not give up meeting together, as some are in the habit of doing, but let us encourage one another." The Bible exhorts us to link ourselves with other Christians. This is especially vital for the man or woman coming out of homosexuality.

Church Involvement

Perhaps you have not been in church for years. Or maybe you attend a church, but nobody knows about your homosexual struggles. You may already have a group of supportive friends but wonder if more people in your church need to know about your sexual struggles.

You may find yourself in the same situation as Tim, the man who wrote this letter: "I'm at the point of total despair. Homosexuality has been a silent struggle in my life. During the past three years, I have succumbed to a double life—playing church on one hand and living as a practicing homosexual on the other. My situation is both overwhelming and futile to me. There is no one in my church that I feel free to confide in about my situation."

If you are like Tim and the thousands of men and women like him, you have four options:

☐ *Keep silent and remain in your church.* Your sexual struggles will probably not change. You will not overcome your homosexuality and eventually will probably drop out of church altogether in discouragement.

☐ *Remain in your church and confide in a church leader.* Over the years, I (Bob) have talked to dozens of pastors and other church leaders who are eager to help members of their congregation who struggle with homosexuality. Often these pastors have not had much experience in dealing with this issue, but they are anxious to learn. Opening up to a pastor, elder or adult Sunday-school teacher may be the best move you ever make in seeking answers.

☐ *Remain in your church and find help outside the church.* For the sake of family (spouse, children) or many other reasons, some ex-gay men and women decide that leaving a church that is not able to help them is not an option, at least for now. For these people the best solution is to find counseling or peer support outside their church. For example, they remain part of a home church for Sunday services but attend a weekly support group for ex-gays or they see a professional counselor at a local Christian agency.

☐ *Look for a new church.* This option should be the last one you consider. Looking for a new church home can be an exhausting, frustrating and time-consuming experience. But if overcoming homosexuality is a major goal during this season of your life, it is worth the investment of time to seek a healthy church home where you can make significant strides forward in your spiritual walk.

Disclosure Issues

Some ex-gays and former lesbians have been surprised by the positive reaction when they told their pastor about their homosexual struggles. Janice joined a local church and became active in ministering to the elderly, which brought her great joy. But as time went by, she felt as if a major part of her life was being carefully hidden from others. This secrecy bothered her.

"I began to experience greater and greater temptations in the area of homosexuality," Janice remembers. "For so long, I had hoped that the Lord would just let me off the hook and I wouldn't have to tell anyone."

Then one night Janice received an unexpected phone call that changed her life. On the other end was a man whom she didn't know. He accused Janice of being a lesbian and threatened physical violence. Janice told the man, "I'm a Christian now," and hung up.

But she was terrified—not so much of what the man might do to her but of her church finding out about her past. All that week the voice on the phone haunted her. Finally in desperation she decided to go and tell her pastor.

She got an unexpected reaction.

"My pastor was very encouraged by my testimony," Janice recalls, "and thought that I should share it with the whole church. I wasn't too excited about that idea."

But, although the pastor's words made her nervous, the more Janice thought and prayed about his proposal, the more she felt convinced that his suggestion was exactly what God wanted her to do.

The day of the service came and Janice felt a deep peace inside. "I knew Jesus was with me. The Holy Spirit gave me the boldness to share my story and the majority of people received it with love. And I felt a freedom in that area of my life that I had wanted for so long."

Janice says that, through the experience of sharing with her church, she discovered the truth of the Scripture, "They overcame him [Satan] by the blood of the Lamb and by the word of their testimony" (Rev 12:11).

John Smid also had many positive experiences when he began telling his church in Omaha, Nebraska, about his homosexual past. John recalls, however, that he also had some fears. "As part of my church's singles' group, I was invited to weekend conferences where I had to share a room and even the same bed with another man in the group.

"I will never forget the first night I slept in the same bed with another guy from church. I lay perfectly still, making sure I didn't cross an imaginary line down the middle. *I don't want Dan to think anything weird is going on,* I thought. *If he knows of my past, he won't want to share a room with me—much less a bed.*"

At first John was cautious about who he told of his past because he was afraid that he would not be invited to events like men's retreats. But he discovered that his fears were groundless. "I found that those who really cared for me as a brother in Christ said my past homosexuality didn't bother them in the least. They were still willing to be my friends."

John felt a great release when he let other men know about his struggles. His friends became his prayer partners as he continued to work through the underlying issues which had led him into homosexuality in the first place.[7]

4

EXPOSING
THE ROOTS

*T*he gigantic coastal California redwoods are fascinating. Each tree seems like a living, breathing giant with a life and personality all its own. When a windstorm or fire topples one of the trees, there is the sense that a "great one" has fallen—especially when you examine the incredible root system that supports these monoliths.

The roots, although shallow, can spread hundreds of feet in every direction, intertwining with the root systems of other giants. The staggering trees that people come to see are only half the story. Beneath the ground lies an entire "forest," providing nourishment and support to the giant redwoods, holding each tree firmly in place.

For a Christian coming out of homosexuality or lesbianism, the homosexual problem may loom as large in your life as a giant redwood: enormous, obvious, unshakable, unchangeable. But just like the root system below the redwood forest, homosexuality also has roots. Many things beneath the surface of our lives feed the gay identity and hold it firmly in place. As these roots are identified and dealt with, through God's leading and in his timing, homosexuality becomes less and less firmly established. Even something as all-encompassing and firmly rooted as a lesbian or homosexual identity will yield to God's patient, persistent, gentle healing.

Why Study Roots?

Before the early 1970s, no ministries were geared specifically for helping people come out of homosexuality. Christians who struggled with gay or lesbian temptations found a measure of healing simply by applying basic Christian disciplines—prayer, Bible study, fellowship—to their lives. Some found the strength to abstain from homosexual activity, but few could see any significant change in the intensity of their homosexual feelings or in the way they viewed themselves. Many believed the best they could hope to be was a bullet-biting, abstinent, Christian homosexual.

Around 1973, specialized ex-gay ministries began to spring up. These groups took a closer look at the question, "Can a homosexual really change?" Former lesbians and gays were not content to bite the bullet, suppressing constant, overwhelming sexual temptations to earn the label "good Christian." If Jesus was real—and they believed he was—they wanted to see his power at work in their lives.

In talking with men and women seeking a way out of homosexuality, leaders of ex-gay ministries began to see common factors in the backgrounds of the people coming for help.

The main areas where these patterns emerged were
☐ early childhood development
☐ family background
☐ temperament and interests
☐ peer pressure
☐ sexual abuse

As individuals started examining these areas of their lives, dealing prayerfully and openly with the feelings and hurts under the surface, they gradually experienced amazing changes.

The stories and insights in this chapter are keys to unlocking the chains of lesbian and homosexual identity, feelings and behavior. We do not look at the roots of homosexual development to dredge up dirt from our childhood or lay blame on our parents. We do it because *understanding homosexual development points the way to true resolution.*

We can look back and see what we are responsible for and what we are not. When we bring to light our own wrong actions and attitudes, we can confess our guilt and receive God's forgiveness. Where we were victims of circumstance and the hurtful actions of other people, we can gain understanding and learn to forgive.

We do not believe that homosexuality is primarily inborn. We base our beliefs on the Bible's teaching about homosexuality, backed up by the lack of conclusive scientific proof for such a theory (see chapter two). But even if homosexual tendencies were an inherited trait, we would not interpret that as an endorsement of gay or lesbian involvement. Many studies have indicated that tendencies toward alcoholism or depression are inherited. But we do not embrace alcoholism and depression as "acceptable alternative" lifestyles. Rather, we try to help people who suffer from these tendencies find healing and recovery.

While we reject the view that homosexuality is genetically determined, we do recognize that the circumstances and pressures that shape a man or woman to conclude "I'm gay" or "I'm a lesbian" can be traced through every stage of an individual's growth and development. Let's look at what can happen in each of these stages: infancy and early childhood, grade school years, puberty and teenage years, and early adulthood.

Sesame Street, Mr. Rogers and Sexual Identity

As soon as we can see, hear and feel—at birth, or even in the womb— we begin taking in information that tells us who we are. Long before we can articulate our feelings or even have an organized thought, we can sense peace, warmth, comfort, love. We can also detect disturbance, tension, anger and fear. We have all heard stories about orphaned infants who have actually died from a lack of holding and warm affection, even when their physical needs for food and shelter were met. God created us as physical, emotional and spiritual beings, and this is evident from the earliest part of our lives. While the events of these early years do not *cause* us to become lesbian or homosexual, they can set the stage for problems to develop later in life.

Ideally, an infant's first year or two of life is spent developing a deep, secure bond of love with the mother that leads to a *healthy sense of personal identity.* Psychologist Erik Erikson calls this the development of "basic trust,"[1] while author and teacher Leanne Payne refers to the process as "coming into a sense of being."[2] With a solid sense of identity and a confidence that his or her needs for love and care will be met, a child has a good foundation for future growth and development.

When this foundation is disrupted, the child is vulnerable to all kinds of problems. Babies who do not achieve "basic trust" see the world as a frightening and unpredictable place. Not having experienced security with their own mothers, they tend to view all new events and people with a negative expectation. Depending on the child's temperament, this can be expressed by withdrawal, apathy and passivity, or by intense aggression and uncontrolled emotion. Infants who do not come into a "sense of being" grow up sensing an inner emptiness or chasm, a "separation anxiety." This can manifest itself later in life through an overwhelming drive to connect with and find their identity in another person.

Failure to achieve "basic trust" or a "sense of being" are conditions found throughout society and do not, in themselves, cause homosexuality or lesbianism. But children who start life lacking this foundation are extraordinarily vulnerable to all developmental disruptions, including those that shape their sexual identities.

While a breakdown in the bond with the mother deeply affects both male and female babies, sexual identity seems to be more noticeably shaped by *disrupted bonding with the same-sex parent:* little girls lacking an intimate attachment to Mom, boys feeling detached and alienated from Dad.[3]

Terri's story illustrates a double dose of this problem: "To begin with, I was adopted. My birth mother was fifteen years old, one of six children. A lot of shame and secrecy surrounded the pregnancy. Her father didn't even know about it; neither did the guy who'd gotten her pregnant. After my birth, I spent a few months in foster homes, and I have no idea what happened to me there. My mom and dad adopted me when I was four months old.

"Recently, my mother gave me my baby book, and I read through it. When I was two, she wrote, 'Terri has only boys to play with, and she is becoming quite rough.' I could tell I was a difficult child to raise. She never told me, 'I love you.' I don't think we ever really connected. I felt more love and affection from my dad, so I identified with him and became his helper, his shadow.

"Often, I was mistaken for a little boy. In my kindergarten picture,

I'm wearing a tie and an army hat. I think my sexual identity was in trouble from an early age."

Young boys can lose their fathers through death or divorce, traumatic events that leave the little boy yearning for love and protection from a man. But many men who struggle with homosexuality grew up with the normal, "nice guy" emotionally distant and detached type of father.

"My dad owned the local Chevrolet dealership," Phil recalls. "People in our little town liked and respected him. My two sisters were born in the early fifties, and I came along a few years later. Dad was so excited to have 'his boy.' He had big dreams of the two of us tossing around a football and catching trout together.

"I wanted to please Dad, but he really wasn't around much. As an adult, I realize how demanding his business was. But as a little boy, I just knew he wasn't there. Then when he did try to play with me, I was shy and uncoordinated. Dad's initial zeal for my maleness quickly turned to embarrassment. I wasn't the son he had bargained for."

Three years after Phil was born, his brother Max came along, and Phil's problems really began. "From the time Max could walk, he looked and acted like a miniature linebacker. I watched Dad's face light up as he threw Max high in the air. 'This is my little boy,' he'd shout while Max let out happy squeals. 'This is my little boy!' So what did that make me? *My daddy doesn't like me,* I would think, my heart aching with shame and disappointment. From then on, I retreated almost exclusively to the company of my mom and my sisters."

Many people experience some degree of rejection in their early years. But when a little boy fails to connect with his dad and a little girl doesn't form a close relationship with her mother, the groundwork is laid for future sexual identity struggles.

Temperament and Interests

Inborn temperament plays an important role too. Boys born with a sensitive, intuitive, artistic nature can be more vulnerable to disruptions in their relationships with their fathers. In fact, if a little boy like this experiences rejection and ridicule from his dad, it's almost a sure bet that he will have sexual identity struggles later on. However, if this "love deficit"[4] is filled by a loving grandfather, stepfather or significantly older brother, the negative effects can be minimized.

What happened to Phil is typical: Mom notices that the son is being rejected (or neglected) by Dad, feels compassion for him and gives him extra love and attention. "Smother mothers" used to be blamed for causing homosexuality in their sons. And it's true that an overly intimate, dominating mother who looks to her son to meet emotional needs not met by her husband can jeopardize her son's masculinity. Most often, however, a mother is just trying to "be there" for the son, to compensate for the dad's absence or disinterest. When the little boy is sensitive to begin with, it then becomes easy for him to model himself after his mother, picking up her mannerisms and the way she expresses herself, and adopting her whole perspective on life. Meanwhile, the boy's hunger for the love, guidance and protection of a man continues to grow.[5]

Inborn temperament and body build affect girls' early development too. Often people expect a young daughter to be soft, sweet and compliant, but some come out of the womb hollering, kicking and looking like they are ready to train for the triathlon. If the girl's parents are also aggressive and athletic, or at least enjoy these characteristics, she probably will grow into a strong, confident heterosexual woman. But sometimes a mother will struggle to accept an aggressive, active daughter, and the little girl will sense her mother's ambivalence. Feeling wounded and rejected, the girl may further detach from her mother, cutting herself off from the source of love she needs to help her grow into her own female identity. In turn, she is left with a same-sex love deficit, leaving her vulnerable to future lesbian involvement.

The Grade School Years: Barbie Versus G.I. Joe

"Sticks and stones may break my bones, but words will never hurt me." Don't we wish this little chant held even one grain of truth! All the scrapes, bruises and broken bones we incurred on the school playground probably are well-healed by now. But the cruel names and nasty remarks hurled at us there can still ring in our ears today, stinging and causing us to wither with shame.

In the grade school years, home and family still play a strong role in shaping our identities, but this is the time when the powerful forces of peer pressure kick in. If the "mold" for our sexual identity is cast in the preschool years, grade school is the period when that mold begins to be filled with wet cement.

A little boy already estranged from his father is now probably getting the same treatment from his peers, along with some nasty labeling and name-calling: "Ralph is a _____" (fill in sissy, fag, femme, wimp, or worse yet, girl).

Rather than face the humiliation sure to be encountered in team sports, Ralph and others like him often develop solitary pursuits: reading, drawing, music, computers, television. They may cultivate girls as their companions, learning to jump rope, volunteering to play house. Or they may team up with other shy and withdrawn boys and even begin some sexual experimentation.

For girls the grade school years often hold powerful events that contribute to later lesbian involvement. In the first few grades a tomboy is not so likely to experience teasing and rejection from other girls. But our sexually oriented culture races children toward premature puberty. By second or third grade most little girls are concerned about being pretty, popular, having the right clothes and giggling about boyfriends. (Actually, much of this is already underway in kindergarten.) The girl who does not share these interests, who truly prefers sports, roughhousing and being buddies with the boys, is starting to feel disconnected from other girls.

Terri recalls getting the message from all the adults around her that she acted more like a boy than a girl. "Isn't she such a tomboy?" they would say.

"It was good-natured," Terri remembers, "but I internalized everything they said. I didn't know who I was. I felt rejected as a girl. It seemed like I should have been born a boy instead."

On the home front girls of this age (between about five and ten) can be encountering other strong patterns that increase vulnerability to future lesbian involvement.

Patty's situation typifies one of these patterns. "I was the oldest of three girls. My dad was a foreman with a local construction company; my mom stayed home and took care of my sisters and me. Dad was hardworking and a good provider, but his mean spirit and explosive temper dominated the household.

"Mom was scared to death of him. She was tiny and thin, never very healthy. Though she was sweet and loving, she never seemed like a parent to us. By the time I was six, she deferred many decisions and much of the care of my sisters to me.

"On weekends, Dad would drink and by late afternoon, the thunderstorm would break. He'd bellow at my mother, 'Emma, you are such an idiot. I knock myself out all week to provide for this family, and you can't even keep the house clean. You're hopeless.'

"My sisters and I got the same treatment. They would cry and cower like my mom. But I would get so mad, I'd feel the heat creeping up through my chest, past my face, until my scalp would tingle and my head would be ready to explode. 'You big jerk!' I would shriek. 'Why don't you just leave us alone?'

"Oddly enough, that would silence him. Soon after my outburst, Dad would slam the front door behind him and head out to the bar or a friend's house for the night. Mom and my sisters would look at me with such admiration. I'd think, *I'm the real protector in this family*. I'd fantasize about my dad's death, how I would get a job and support my mom and my sisters. *Men!* I thought. *Who needs them?*"

In contrast Mary was an only child, sheltered and protected by both her parents, who were in their forties when she was born. "My whole family was governed by the fear of taking risks. Dad worked in the bank's loan department for years, and until I was born Mom clerked in a florist shop. They never thought they could have kids and were thrilled when I was born.

"But they were terrified of something happening to their 'little girl,' and I internalized all their phobias. I hated the playground games, rough boys—even the neighborhood gang of girls seemed too wild and frightening to me. By second grade I was so withdrawn that no one wanted to play with me. I liked my safe little world with Mom and Dad, but an enormous loneliness took root in my heart. I yearned for friendship, but it seemed completely out of reach for me. I think this isolation helped set me up to fall later into emotional dependency and eventually, lesbian relationships."

Sexual Abuse

While family dynamics, temperament and peer pressure strongly shape a person's sexual identity, the single factor that most powerfully propels a girl toward a lesbian identity is sexual abuse: incest, rape or molestation.

Sexual abuse encompasses *any* kind of sexual interchange between a child and anyone bigger, stronger or older. The spectrum of abusive behavior ranges from a lingering stare, with or without verbal comments, to inappropriate touching, kissing, oral sex and anal or vaginal intercourse.

Incest, which we define as sexual contact with a family member, relative or regular caretaker, is the most common and damaging form of sexual abuse. Usually, the perpetrator is a male—a father, stepfather, uncle or older brother—although women can be abusers too.

Incest wreaks incredible devastation because a child is betrayed and violated by the very people she should be trusting to care for and protect her. Often the molested child will think, *I must be a horrible person for something like this to happen to me!* The abuser may threaten to harm or even kill the child if she ever divulges "our secret."

Unable to deal with the trauma of such events, the child may minimize the abuse or even repress it completely. The tremendous volume of rage, hurt and indignation goes underground, emerging later in a variety of choices, one of which for women might be a total rejection of men and a turning exclusively to women for love and affirmation.

Here, Barbara tells her story: "Our family looked pretty ordinary on the outside. Mom was a nurse who supervised the 3:00 p.m. to 11:00 p.m. shift at the hospital. She was a chipper, brisk, busy lady—not one to dwell much on emotions. I admired her and wanted to be like her, but I never felt like she really saw me. It seemed like I never had enough of her attention, her hugs, or her encouragement."

Barbara's father was a science teacher and baseball coach. An only child, Barbara would walk over to her dad's office after school to ride home with him. In the spring he would take her along to baseball practice. "Dad was more huggy and kissy than Mom," she remembers. "I felt a lot closer to him."

In the summer between fifth and sixth grades, Barbara started to mature physically. "I wore baggy shirts and jeans, hoping no one would notice these changes. Dad started acting more distant. At times I would catch him staring at me in a strange way."

One night, Barbara was stretched out on the couch watching television. Her mother was working, and she was home alone with her father. "Dad came in and asked if he could sit down next to me. I moved my legs to make room for him. He sat down, then took my legs and stretched them back out across his lap, patting my knees. At first, this seemed nice, but as we watched the movie, he began running his hands up and down my legs. When I got nervous and sat up straight, he laughed and said, 'What's wrong? Can't I even show love to my little girl anymore?' "

Things progressed from there. "Dad began telling me how lonely he was and how he needed me to keep him company while Mom was at work. I didn't know what to think! I was lonely, too, and while the affection from my dad made me uncomfortable, I didn't want to upset him or make him mad at me."

Gradually the evenings on the couch progressed to more touching, then kissing. "When I reached junior high, I looked like I was about nineteen. Dad told me it was his job as a father to teach me about love, about sex. He did, in every way."

The incest continued for three years. Barbara hated and despised her sexual relationship with her father. She felt like a "total freak, outwardly pretending to be a normal kid, inwardly feeling like my father's real wife."

Much of Barbara's hatred was directed at her mother. *How can she abandon me to Dad like this?* she wondered. *Can't she see what's going on?* When Barbara would yell and curse at her mother over insignificant things, her father would defend her: "Barbara's just a typical teenager—all teenage girls fight with their mothers." *True enough,* Barbara screamed inside. *But not all teenage girls have sex with their fathers.*

"As I spent more time with my friends at school, I realized how bizarre and horrible my situation was with Dad. Instead of pitying him I started threatening to tell Mom if the sexual advances continued. And I started staying out late almost every night, studying at the library or at a friend's house. My main goal was to survive until graduation, when I could get away for good."

Barbara's sexual experiences with her father profoundly influenced her sexual identity, causing her to associate heterosexual desire with feelings of shame and violation. We'll look at the conclusion to Barbara's story later in this chapter.

Sexual abuse greatly impacts an individual's sexual identity on many levels. In chapter ten, we will examine the dynamics and resolution of this issue, which affects many men as well.

Junior High and High School: Attack of the Hormones
The onset of puberty can be like the last chapter of a mystery novel:

finally you discover what all these clues have been leading up to!

Most people from a lesbian or gay background feel different or may even be labeled "queer" from an early age. But the full significance of these labels hits, usually in the junior high years, when the first strong rushes of sexual attraction come surging up—and turn out to be surging in the wrong direction.

Tom remembers how girls were his closest friends during grade school. "I played jacks, house, jump rope—everything they did—and I was good at all of them. Girls felt safe and comfortable. Boys seemed alien and intimidating. So in junior high most boys were becoming interested in girls who seemed different and fascinating to them. To me, girls were familiar. Boys were different and fascinating, and my feelings of sexual attraction went out to them."

At age twelve when Tom concluded that he was a homosexual, he decided never to tell anyone about his discovery. He prayed that the feelings would be a "passing phase" that would eventually go away.

Even though our culture is superficially more tolerant of homosexuality than it once was, most high school kids do not want to be gay. Most teenagers who discover same-sex attractions take Tom's approach: repress them, ignore them and hope they will go away. Even those who act out homosexually resist accepting the label "gay." Some get into opposite-sex dating in hopes of drowning out their homosexual feelings. (Many boys and girls experiment homosexually during grade school and junior high. This in no way means they will be homosexual, and usually their *feelings* of sexual attraction are directed heterosexually.)

During childhood Janine Puls, a clinical social worker and former group leader with Desert Stream Ministries in Los Angeles, suffered abuse from older boys and men on several occasions. Despite her fears, she began going on dates during high school. But these heterosexual relationships only seemed to bring more hurt and pain. Janine remembers one night in particular: "I had a date to go to a dance. It was very classy, a special night around San Francisco Bay on a boat. I bought a new dress for it. Then, at the last minute, my date called and canceled. I was so hurt, I shut down emotionally. I decided, 'I'm not going to be open to men for dates after this.'" This experience gave Janine one more push in the direction of same-sex relationships. Eventually she abandoned men completely, leaving her vulnerable to lesbian relationships.

Throughout junior high and high school, Jack laughed and joked along with other boys about girls and sex, but secretly, he felt very little sexual attraction toward women. He hoped "the right girl" would come along and cure him of his lack of interest.

"Through my involvement on the school yearbook staff, I met Cindy, and we started dating. We double-dated with another couple who worked on the yearbook. They were having sex, so Cindy and I started sleeping together too. When I realized I didn't enjoy being sexually involved with Cindy, I got really depressed. I had to admit to myself that I was much more sexually drawn to men than to women. My disappointment with Cindy confirmed what I'd begun to suspect since my early teens: I must be gay."

College and Beyond

The last step in the development of a lesbian or homosexual identity usually comes in the decade after high school, when all kinds of options are spread before us. Away from the restraining influences of parents and the people we grew up with, many of us use the post-high school years to try anything in the search for our life's direction and identity.

For young adults, going to college or becoming involved in the working world opens up a variety of avenues for self-expression. If a woman has any inclination toward lesbian feelings, now is the time she is likely to "go for it." Other women stop short of physical involvement but form inappropriately close and exclusive relationships with other women, which are referred to as "emotional dependencies" (see chapter nine). College roommates, feminist groups, women's athletics, the drama department, campus Christian ministries, you name it— women we have talked to have found their first lover in all these places. And, despite military regulations, the armed services provide a natural setting for coming out into the lesbian lifestyle.

Here is what happened to Barbara, who escaped her father's unwelcome advances when she left home after high school: "In college, I tried dating men, but being with men brought up the feelings of shame and revulsion I connected with Dad. I found myself drawn to female friends who were competent and aggressive, like my mom. But I looked for women who, unlike Mom, offered me sympathy, attention, emotional support."

By the end of her freshman year Barbara was involved in her first lesbian relationship. "While being with a man felt strange and uncomfortable, being with a woman felt wonderfully normal to me, like I was finally getting what I needed."

For most men the biggest post-high school decision is whether or not to "come out" and be openly identified as gay, or to maintain a straight image while either secretly *acting out* (getting involved in homosexual behavior) or trying to suppress homosexual feelings altogether.

"In high school I anguished over my sexual feelings," Rick remembers. "I hated the thought of being homosexual, so I dated girls and tried sports, though I wasn't very athletic. Anything to hide what I was going through. When I got to college, a gay group had an office in the student union. I started walking by there, looking in casually at first. I didn't want anyone to know I was interested."

A few weeks later Rick was having lunch in the snack bar on campus. "One of the leaders from the gay group walked up to my table and said, 'I'm Jim. Do you mind if I sit with you?' I almost choked on my cheeseburger. But he sat down anyway. After a few minutes of general conversation, he said, 'I've seen you around. And I don't know if you'd be interested, but my roommate and I are having a party tonight. Here's our address.'

"He wrote a few lines on a piece of paper and dropped it on my tray. 'See you later, I hope,' he said, and walked out of the snack bar. I was terrified—and thrilled."

Following an afternoon of agonizing internal debate, Rick drove to the address scribbled on that piece of paper. "My palms were sweating and my heart was pounding. I walked up and rang the doorbell. Jim opened the door and grinned. 'Come in,' he said. And I did. That night, I walked right out of one life and into another."

These examples are just a few of the ways men and women make the decision, "I am gay" or "I'm lesbian." Pressures from our culture, from individuals we meet and from our own internal vulnerabilities converge to move us toward that declaration. Once people are in the lifestyle, getting out becomes more and more unthinkable.

What would induce any of us to leave behind a world that is comfortable and accepting (at least on the surface), a world that seems to meet all our emotional, social and sexual needs? That's a good question. In the next chapter we will look at some people who decided to leave homosexuality and learn why they attempted such a radical change.

5

SAYING
GOODBY

*O*ne of the most exciting moments in the movie The Wizard of Oz occurs when the tornado lifts Dorothy, Toto and the house up from stark, plain, black-and-white Kansas and drops them in Oz. Dorothy takes a moment to collect herself after landing with such a big thud. Then she cautiously opens the door and peeps out at a whole new world of . . . color!

For some people, coming to Christ is like landing in Oz. Ordinary, humdrum existence is suddenly suffused with vibrant new color and meaning.

But many people who are leaving behind the lesbian or gay lifestyle to follow Christ feel like they are experiencing *Wizard of Oz* in reverse. Their commitment to do God's will has whirled them away from the zany, stimulating, multi-hued world of the lifestyle and plopped them down in the flat, sparse, black-and-white plains of Christianity.

Bill Hernandez, director of The Healing Center at the Vineyard Christian Fellowship in San Francisco, remembers what he experienced when he left the gay lifestyle in 1978.

"I had been at what many gays would consider to be the top of the lifestyle back then. My lover, Grant, was handsome, calm, very masculine and financially stable. And he was committed to me. He wanted a lifetime partnership.

"We lived in a penthouse with a panoramic view of Lake Merritt in Oakland, the city lights twinkling in the background. Our apartment was beautiful: thick, spotless white carpeting; sparkling, tiled kitchen; rich, oak furniture.

"Our situation, in many ways, was ideal—except it wasn't. I had become a Christian at U. C. Berkeley, before I went into the lifestyle. Now I knew God was calling me to come back to him. I was getting glimpses of the gay lifestyle, how foolish and destructive it really was. I knew being gay was holding me back in my relationship with Jesus and, as comfortable as I was with Grant, I needed to get out."

Bill worked with Nancy, a Christian woman who frequently told him about her church in nearby San Rafael that had a ministry to people coming out of homosexuality. "My ears perked up at that," Bill recalls. "Thinking I was revealing my deepest secret, I told Nancy, 'You know, I am from that background.' She just looked at me and said, 'I knew it all along.' "

Bill called the ministry and made plans to visit one of their group meetings. He drove across the Richmond-San Rafael bridge and began to search for the meeting place, an apartment located above a health food store.

"I parked my car, walked past an overflowing dumpster reeking of garbage and up some creaking, sagging stairs that needed a coat of paint. At the top of the stairs stood an old, cracked mirror smeared with mud. My mind flashed back to the gleaming, floor-to-ceiling mirrors covering one wall of our bedroom in the penthouse. *Maybe I should leave now,* I thought, but something inside me urged me on.

"I walked into a living room filled with mismatched, dilapidated furniture. Several people were there: Cindy, dressed in a black polyester cowboy suit with white stitching, looking tough, strumming a guitar, with one pointed boot up on the couch; Craig, a middle-aged man with light brown hair, studying me with piercing eyes; Jim, the Bible study leader, dripped with gold chains and gestured flamboyantly.

"I walked across the room and sat down next to a young, dark-haired man with intense brown eyes who was soaking his bandaged hand in a bucket of ice water. 'I'm Paul,' he said. 'What happened to your hand?' I asked. 'Oh,' he said. 'Last night, my homosexual temptations were so bad, I put my fist through the wall.' "

Bill glanced around the room, contrasting the scene before him with his white-carpeted penthouse and "perfect" lover in Oakland. "I hated to admit it, but something here in this depressing room with its strange inhabitants was drawing me. For the first time in months I felt peace inside. It seemed like God was saying, 'This is where I want you to be.' "

Grief and Disorientation

Any time we lose something or someone important to us, the loss registers deep within our being. When this loss greatly impacts our life, we grieve. For people coming out of homosexuality the loss can be multifaceted: a network of friends, an identity, possibly a lover, a secure living situation, hopes of having a romantic or sexual relationship (at least, the kind we prefer). The change is often dramatic and total, and the grief that follows can be devastating.

If you are at the point of making this step or if you have recently left the gay or lesbian lifestyle, you need to give yourself permission to grieve. This can be a critical step in your healing. As Christians, we make a serious mistake when we glibly convey the message "If you have faith in God, he will get you through anything. Just praise the Lord through your trials."

When others view the lifestyle or relationship you are leaving behind as sinful or negative, they may find it hard to acknowledge your need to mourn. Straight Christians often cannot imagine why you enjoyed the homosexual lifestyle in the first place; they assume you are glad to be rid of it. They may not understand *at all* why an evening at Bible study does not excite you as much as an evening with your lesbian or gay friends.

Please do not let guilt and outside pressures deprive you of your need to mourn those things that you miss. God wants to minister to the hurts and needs you bring before him.

TIME OUT

Write down what you miss about your past homosexual relationships. Ask God to replace these longings with his new desires for your life.

The Christian life and your growing relationship with God *will* provide times of excitement, joy, comfort and peace. But there will still be tears and loneliness, hours or even days of anxiety or depression. These times need to be accepted and experienced as a normal part of making any major life change.

"After I left the lifestyle," Bill Hernandez recalls, "I dealt with depression and denial for about two years. On one hand, God was blessing me, teaching me about himself and his Word in amazing ways. Basically I had peace. But about every six weeks I would get antsy—anxiety and loneliness would build up inside of me and I would get headaches. I missed my lover and deep down inside, I would call his name. I would think, *Only Grant can help me get over this feeling.*"

For the first few months after leaving the lifestyle, Bill made occasional trips across the bay to visit his ex-lover. "Usually we'd become sexually involved again. Every time this happened, I felt devastated and worthless. But I would turn to the Lord with my feelings. He didn't condemn me. He would forgive me and fill me with new hope."

Bill recalls, "The more of God's love I experienced, the more confident I became. Eventually the trips to my ex-lover stopped altogether. The security and peace I had in Jesus were more real to me than anything homosexual involvement could offer."

Emotional Ups and Downs

Donna had similar experiences during her first months after becoming a Christian and leaving the lesbian lifestyle. "I moved out from my lover's apartment and came to live with a Christian couple I knew. I had my own room in their basement, and I spent a lot of time down there, playing my guitar, praying, singing and sometimes crying.

"I was on a roller coaster. One day I would wake up bursting with enthusiasm, enjoying such an awareness of God's presence that I would be on a high all day. I was constantly sharing the Lord with people at the medical lab where I worked. The next day I would be driving along the freeway and a song would come on the radio like 'You Needed Me' by Anne Murray. Thoughts and images of my ex-lover would rise up before me and I would be devastated. Tears would stream down my face, and I'd pray that I wouldn't get in a car accident. Then the rest of the day I would be swimming in memories, longing for my past life.

"Thank God, I had Mark and Christine, the couple I lived with, to unload on. They accepted me whether I was up or down, and I think my ups were sometimes harder to take than my downs. Their love and commitment pulled me through those first rough months."

Donna's turbulent emotions are not unusual during the first months, or even years, of leaving homosexuality behind. These feelings are bewildering because they fluctuate so wildly, even violently.

Sometimes the new excitement and freedom can be heady and euphoric. Phil recalls, "When I first left the lifestyle, I experienced real freedom from homosexual desires. I'd hear stories of how people would fall back into homosexual activity, and I would pity them. I felt so free, I wanted to tell everyone, 'You don't have to be gay! Jesus can set you free—he did it for me.' I actually did go back and treat some of my gay friends to my enthusiastic message of hope. They thought I'd lost it completely."

Phil's gay desires returned weeks later, sometimes with incredible intensity. While he did not act on these feelings and he was able to turn to Christian friends and to the Lord for support, he said, "I definitely got off my high horse."

HIV and AIDS
One of the most terrifying aspects of dealing with past homosexual involvement—especially for men—is the question of whether or not you have become infected with the HIV virus. Any sexual activity which has involved the exchange of bodily fluids exposes an individual (male or female) to the risk of infection. And researchers know that the virus can reside in a person's body for ten years or more before the onset of the symptomatic phase of HIV disease (such as ARC and AIDS).

Should ex-gays be tested for HIV? Most health experts recommend it, as evidence is mounting that early intervention delays the onset of overt illness. Also, even though taking the test probably represents your greatest fear, living with the dread of uncertainty for years is counterproductive to a joyful, peaceful existence. Knowing your HIV status allows you to make appropriate lifestyle changes, such as altering your diet and exercise regimen. It also enables you, if appropriate, to share this fact with your family and closest friends who can give you emotional support in facing the uncertainties of the future. We feel that it's *essential* to know your HIV status if you're married, or if you are interested in pursuing a dating relationship.

Dealing with Your Ex

Do I have to leave my lover? This may be a major concern at this point if you have been involved in a significantly long-term relationship. You may even have stopped the sexual aspect of your relationship. But now you wonder, *Must we separate, or can we remain friends?*

Here's how one man expressed the dilemma: "I am trying to change my gay life, but I'm almost forty years old. I am living with another man, and I love him. We both want to stay together as Christians for support and companionship, but change our sexual ways. I feel we can do this, though everyone is against it. Can it work?"

This is a very important decision. There are principles in the Word of God which will help you in knowing what to do. First of all, your spiritual life is the first priority for your life as a Christian. Anything that comes between you and God must be removed. Are you growing as a Christian through this friendship or are you slipping back into old habits and feelings through its influence?

Does your friend share your commitment to leaving homosexuality? The Scriptures warn about "having fellowship" with those who reject God's truth (see 2 Cor 6:14). This not only includes living together but also having a close friendship. Is your friend following God or living in disobedience? "Keep away from every brother who is idle and does not live according to the teaching you received from us," says Paul in 2 Thessalonians 3:6.

If you and your ex-lover are still falling into sexual immorality—even infrequently—then separation is mandatory. The Bible commands us to "flee from sexual immorality" (1 Cor 6:18).

This principle also applies to emotional entanglements which are excessive. One of the danger signs is exclusivity: if both you and your ex-lover are not pursuing *significant* relationships with others (especially same-sex friends), then your continued friendship is detrimental and must be severed. Another danger sign is falling into inappropriate expressions of affection (such as kissing, long embraces, body massages or necking and petting types of behavior). Your needs for affection and friendship are legitimate, but these are not healthy ways in which to have them met.

Are you able to be open about this friendship with others? If you are hiding certain aspects of the relationship with other friends ("We're doing great," you say, although you are barely able to refrain from sexual involvement), then the relationship is probably headed for disaster. Your relationship should be open to the scrutiny of others, especially a pastor or counselor with experience in ex-gay issues. Your situation may appear harmless to you, but outsiders have the advantage of objectivity. They may see dynamics and effects in your relationship that are invisible to you.

Should you and your former lover separate? There is no simple answer that fits all situations. Give this matter considerable thought and prayer, and seek spiritual counsel. Probably no other decision in the first months of your commitment to leave homosexuality will have such an impact on your success or failure.

Loneliness

Making a decision to follow Christ—or to leave the homosexual lifestyle or a lover as a part of that decision—can bring an interesting paradox: the end of one kind of loneliness and the beginning of another.

When I (Lori) first asked Christ to come into my life, I was surprised by a radical change within myself. While growing up basically as an agnostic, I had battled a terrible sense of alienation. I felt different and apart from God and from other people, even—or maybe, especially—my closest friends. This was not a feeling I articulated; it just gurgled below the surface of my life, coloring my outlook and influencing all my decisions.

When I was nineteen, I asked Christ to come into my heart because I believed it was the right thing to do. What an unexpected bonus to discover that my inner bleakness and isolation vanished like frost melting in the mid-morning sun. Jesus was within, dwelling in me by the power of the Holy Spirit. Whereas solitude once meant being alone with my own thoughts, now it became an opportunity for fellowship of the richest kind—with the Lord. Being alone did not automatically mean being lonely.

But there was another side to all this. I needed friends! I needed new places to go, people to be with. One of my best friends had become a Christian at the same time I did, which was comforting. But Linda seemed to be doing better at being a Christian than I was. We were both nineteen, working at the newspaper in our small Minnesota hometown. Before we became Christians, we had both had an active social life that revolved around the homes of our non-Christian friends, but more particularly, the K-V Bar and Lounge, a local tavern where people our age gathered to hang out, drink beer and socialize. Now I am not saying that a Christian should never go into a bar. But Linda and I both knew that if we were going to avoid old friendships and activities that were unhealthy for us, our regular attendance at the K-V would have to stop.

I recall one Friday around 9:00 p.m., not many weeks after we had prayed to receive Christ. Linda and I were at her home, doing needlepoint and watching television. I could imagine the crowd at the K-V really starting to pick up. Some of my old friends from high school probably would be home for the weekend. And what about that guy, Dave, I had talked to there a few weeks ago? Probably he was at the K-V right now, looking around for me. I glanced over at Linda, who was serenely stitching away. Suddenly, I burst into tears.

"I want to go to the bar," I said, sobbing. Linda looked at me sympathetically and said, "I know how badly you feel. It grieves me, too, when I'm tempted to do things I know God wouldn't like." I looked back at her, incredulous, and said, "I am not grieved because I am tempted to do something God wouldn't like. I'm grieved because I want to go to the bar—and you won't go with me."

Hidden Power in Loneliness

Loneliness is such a pervasive part of making any life change, especially coming out of homosexuality or lesbianism. It can seem like your worst enemy, stalking you at any unguarded moment, threatening to do you in. The secret of loneliness is that it holds one of the most powerful keys to a changed life. Rather than being your worst enemy, it can become your ally as you seek to change and grow.

Our willingness to endure loneliness—experience the feeling of leaving the known for the unknown, walk through unfamiliar, sometimes hostile territory, alone, yet not alone, full of fears, yet trusting in God—this is the bridge we cross to arrive at new life in Christ.

This journey through loneliness is one facet of what the Bible calls "dying to self." We let go of the old so the new might come (Col 3:9-10). The seed of our old lifestyle, our former security, goes into the ground and dies so that our new life might be raised up (Jn 12:24).

On the other hand, I (Lori) don't believe we should endure more loneliness than we have to. When loneliness strikes, depression, lethargy and self-pity often come with it. Here are a collection of ways other people have dealt with loneliness.

☐ *Plan ahead for weekends.* One woman said, "By midweek, I start making plans for the weekend, not just to fill the hours but to do things I really enjoy. I arrange with friends to hang out and watch television, get tickets for a concert or go out to dinner. If I wait until Friday night to make plans, I'm too tired to initiate anything. Also, if a friend says 'no' to my suggestion, it hurts my feelings less to hear that 'no' on Wednesday than it does on Friday."

☐ *Adopt a new attitude toward time alone.* Look forward to it—schedule it in. Have a collection of "things I can't wait to do when I get time alone." Realize your own company, as well as the company of Jesus, is some of the best you'll ever have.

☐ *Listen to music.* Stretch out on the couch or on the floor, put the headphones on and really get into it.

☐ *Read.* I (Lori) love to read. When Christ returns, I am sure that I'll be reading. It helps to have several books lined up for that night alone so at least one of them will spark your interest.

☐ *Treat yourself as someone special.* When eating alone, don't just heat up a TV dinner (unless that's what you crave) but prepare a nice meal, set a place mat, light a candle. Thank the Lord for your meal and invite him to join you.

☐ *Make your home a real nest.* Invest time, effort and money (it doesn't take much) in making your living area feel warm and inviting. Look for ways to express creativity and individuality in your home: build a beautiful wooden bookshelf to house your favorite volumes; creatively display any collections or hobbies: art, rock collecting, photography, etc.

☐ *Catch up on telephone calls and letter writing.*

☐ *Use time alone to strengthen family relationships,* by calling, writing or, if possible, visiting in person.

☐ *Go shopping.* One rainy Friday night, I (Lori) had the best time shopping. I splurged on a great pair of Frye boots which became a staple of my wardrobe. People who knew me ten years ago still remember those boots.

☐ *Browse in bookstores.* Life simply never holds enough time to linger in a bookstore, poring over interesting volumes, collecting ideas, savoring the aroma of new books. A bookstore with a coffee shop is better yet.

☐ *Exercise.* Work out at the gym, go for a jog or take a pleasant, leisurely walk.

☐ *Call someone and see if you can come over.* Rent a movie and bring a snack.

☐ *Look for a singles' group, support group or Bible study,* which are often scheduled on Friday or Saturday evenings. If you find one that genuinely interests you, commit to a group like this. It can be a great springboard for socializing.

☐ *Invite someone to go to a movie with you,* perhaps even a person you would not normally consider asking.

☐ *Take a nap or go to bed early.*

☐ *Clean house.* If you can get the initial momentum going, you'll be shocked at how thoroughly you will clean and organize major areas of your living space. This always leads to a good, energized feeling afterward.

☐ *Go for a drive.*

☐ *Read the Sunday newspaper at a coffee shop.*

☐ *Explore garage sales and flea markets.* You never know what great bargains and interesting curios you will uncover.

☐ *Play music.* Practice your favorite instrument. Play your guitar and sing. Teach yourself new chords.

☐ *Look for chances to serve others.* There are abundant opportunities in your neighborhood for ministering to children, singles, elderly citizens, or single parents. Check your local social service agencies for volunteer opportunities.

☐ Finally, or maybe foremost, *cultivate your relationship with the Lord.* Pray, immerse yourself in the Bible, read Christian classics, meditate on Scripture or on God's character—just "hang out" and relax in God's presence. These are great things to do when you are lonely or even when you're not. Your present relationship with the Lord sets down the foundation for what is to come. Don't let these opportunities for time alone with God slip by.

When we recognize that loneliness is unavoidable—and that we are not alone in being lonely—we can relax with it. In walking through the lonely times we grow. And as we grow, we become equipped to minister to others with sensitivity and understanding.

Time of Transition

During this stage in your life hold onto one important thought: it's temporary. Will life always be this way? Of course not. Will you always feel this way? Not at all! You are in a transition stage. Any major life change is stressful. Your grief, loneliness and other emotions are normal. These feelings you are experiencing are real and valid, but they will not last forever.

Several years ago I (Bob) underwent major abdominal surgery for an inborn defect in my bowel. When I woke up, I felt marvelous—until the anesthetic wore off. Then I began buzzing the nurses every three hours for a shot of morphine. Talk about pain! It was excruciating when the dressings were changed or when I stood up and took my first halting steps the next day. It took months to get my strength back and feel normal again. Now I can barely remember the agony of that recovery period.

Leaving homosexuality is something akin to major spiritual surgery. You may have left a strong social network. Your identity is in turmoil. Your whole world has been turned upside-down (or maybe right-side up!). In any case the emotions churning inside are par for the course. Allow yourself to experience them, but don't allow yourself to imagine that life will always be like this. It won't. Or that what you have left behind is ultimately better. It isn't.

6

BREAKING
ADDICTIVE PATTERNS

*C*liff *was about ten years old when he saw his first pornographic* magazine. It happened in the basement of a neighbor's house, where a fourteen-year-old boy showed the magazine to several younger boys.

After that experience Cliff began noticing similar magazines at the local drugstore. By the time he was fifteen he was sneaking a quick look through the current issue of *Playgirl,* aware that he was far more interested in looking at photos of men than women. He was also regularly indulging in masturbation, using the pictures he had seen in magazines to feed his fantasies.

The struggle with masturbation and pornography remained a pattern in Cliff's life for the next decade. During that time he was a faithful church member. He graduated from a large Christian college, and then was hired as a full-time minister of music at a large suburban church. But all his spiritual activities did not seem to affect his powerful homosexual desires.

Many times Cliff vowed to quit looking at pornography. His resolve usually lasted a week or two, then he would go back to his old patterns. One time he refrained for six months, then found an old magazine in a department store restroom. The next week Cliff found himself in an adult bookstore, looking for the current issue of the same magazine he had found in the bathroom.

One Saturday night Cliff rented his first adult video. After that his resistance vanished, and he began watching several X-rated movies each week. Cliff desperately wanted to stop his sexual sin, but he was hooked—just like many other men and women coming out of homosexuality and lesbianism.

The Dilemma of Sexual Feelings

How do men and women control their sexual behavior? Is it really possible to stop impure thoughts? How do we find purity in our sexual desires when we have indulged in homosexual relationships for many years?

"I couldn't imagine my life without a lover, or without a sexual relationship," confessed Maggie, who had been involved in the lesbian lifestyle over a ten-year period. "The times when I was in between partners were agonizing. I would have one-night stands, sometimes even with men. When I first left the lifestyle, I realized I might have to live without sex for the rest of my life. But that was too depressing to think about."

Why doesn't God just wipe out all our sexual desires, like pulling the plug from a wall socket? Because our sexuality is an integral part of our humanness, which he has declared "good" (Gen 1:31). Our sexual longings have become distorted, but they are, nevertheless, a marvelous creation and wonderful part of who we are as human beings.

Our sexuality draws us out of isolation. We were created for fellowship with other humans—and part of that companionship in marriage is sexual. "It is not good for the man to be alone," God said about Adam, and he created Eve as a companion (Gen 2:18). Sexual neutrality would make for a dull world.

So it is helpful to remember that *our sexual drive is good, not evil.* We can easily fall into the error of seeing our sexual feelings as "the enemy," an unfortunate part of our being that keeps us defeated in our Christian walk. *If I could only be asexual, with no sexual drive,* we may think, *then I could really be a mature Christian.* But God does not give us a partial lobotomy, then call us stable Christians because we no longer experience certain temptations.

Maturity comes as we learn to control our sexuality. Just as our body's muscles are strengthened by exercise, so our spiritual strength is built up by exercising self-control and maturity in our sexual choices.

Here is another key insight: *Our homosexual and lesbian feelings point to deeper emotional needs.* Over the years I (Bob) have asked many people overcoming homosexuality what drew them into lesbian or gay relationships. Many of them admitted that they were not primarily interested in sex, although that could certainly be one factor. Usually these people listed other reasons: wanting attention from others, seeking affirmation, desiring companionship, avoiding boredom, feeling close to someone else, seeking excitement.

Most of these reasons are nonsexual. They are social and emotional. *Therefore these needs can potentially be met through nonsexual relationships.* In fact, because homosexuality is, at its root, a symptom of unmet emotional needs, we will continue to struggle with homosexual feelings until these emotional longings are fulfilled.

Ultimately our deepest needs are met through our relationship with God. He has created us that way; no human being can reach deep inside us like he can, to meet our core needs for communion and intimacy with another. Then we need people to meet other social and emotional needs for companionship and friendship. These needs are universal and powerful. They *must* be met before we will find freedom in our sexuality (we will talk more about forming close, healthy same-sex relationships in chapter nine). Until these emotional needs are satisfied, we will continue to struggle with inappropriate sexual desires.

Temptation Versus Sin

Is it a sin to have homosexual or lesbian feelings? Does God condemn you for being attracted to other members of your own sex? No, being tempted is not the same as sin. God does not condemn us for our feelings.

All men and women have sexual feelings. All of us experience sexual attractions daily. Married people may be attracted to individuals other than their spouse. Are these feelings sinful?

The Bible distinguishes carefully between such feelings and sin.

Inappropriate feelings, in biblical terminology, fit into the category of "temptation." Temptations are not sin. Being sexually attracted to another person is not the same as "committing adultery in your heart" (see Mt 5:28). For it to become sin, you have to act on the temptation, either in your mind or body.

Many, if not most, men and women coming out of homosexuality tend to forget this important distinction between temptation and sin. They suffer from continual condemnation, feeling dragged down, thinking that God is disapproving of them because of their same-sex feelings or attractions. Nothing could be further from the truth. God understands our struggles. He knows that our sexual energy does not suddenly turn on when we enter into marriage and stay focused on our spouse for the rest of our life.

All Christians have to deal with inappropriate sexual feelings and attractions. Those of us overcoming homosexuality are not unique; we do not belong in a different subclass than the rest of the church. Sexual struggles are a part of being human!

Jesus, in his humanity, experienced temptation. Even sexual temptation. "For we do not have a high priest [Jesus] who is unable to sympathize with our weaknesses, but we have one who has been tempted *in every way* just as we are—yet without sin" (Heb 4:15, emphasis added). This passage makes a clear distinction between *temptation* (something that Jesus experienced) and *sin* (something he did not do).

When do homosexual or lesbian temptations become sin? The book of James sheds light on this important question: "But each one is tempted when, by his own evil desire, he is dragged away and enticed. Then, *after desire has conceived, it gives birth to sin*" (Jas 1:14-15, emphasis added). There is always a time gap between conception and birth. A homosexual thought occurring in our mind can be either killed or nurtured. If it grows, it gives birth to sin. That is where our ability to choose comes into effect.

We can choose whether or not homosexual thoughts (temptations) will become sin. If we nurture them, they will grow into lust. Simply defined, lust is the desire to have what is not rightfully mine. Another person's body does not belong to me. Therefore it is not my right to use that individual's body to bring me sexual pleasure.

Of course, lust can involve much more than just sex. We can lust for emotional intimacy and seek it by forming relationships that avoid genital sex but are riddled with deep and exclusive emotional bonds that are inappropriate.

We can even lust for "good things" like marriage and children. Such life experiences can be wonderful, but we won't possess them unless God gives them to us.

We can even lust for something else that seems good: a total absence of homosexual or lesbian feelings. "If I can't be totally healed," some people have told us, "then I'm not interested at all!" What a tragic error. This type of "all-or-nothing" thinking does not take into account that coming out of homosexuality is a *process*. As we persevere, God will reward us with growth and maturity. But these qualities take time to develop; they come through persistence and perseverance. Change comes slowly, like the sun slowly moving across the sky. We must be patient with ourselves—and with the process of recovery.

Back to Roots

Homosexual or lesbian feelings are not sin. However, this does not mean we should simply accept our homosexual feelings as a "thorn in the flesh" and not seek to overcome them. As we have seen, homosexual desires often are a symptom of unmet emotional needs. So begin getting those needs met through appropriate relationships. Why settle for sexual frustration when you can have emotional fulfillment instead?

In chapter four we discussed some common patterns in the lives of men and women who have grown up to experience inappropriate same-sex longings. Understanding these patterns is merely theoretical, unless we begin to take steps to fill the underlying emotional and relational needs that gave rise to our struggles with homosexuality.

Filling those underlying needs will not automatically eradicate your homosexual or lesbian desires. Other factors (including wrong thought patterns and spiritual warfare), which we will discuss in the next chapter, are operating to keep them alive. However, many men and women find that their homosexual or lesbian desires *decrease in intensity* when their emotional needs are being satisfied through healthy relationships. The deeper and more emotionally satisfying these relationships, the less we will be tempted to meet those emo-

tional needs through inappropriate sexual acts or emotional dependencies.

Coping with Sexual Temptation

We cannot avoid sexual stimulation in our culture—unless we hide
at home with a bag over our heads! Today sexual stimuli are every-
where we look—television, movies, magazines and newspapers. Our
local paper in San Francisco has even taken its readers into the back
rooms of lesbian sadomasochism bars.

So what do we do?

☐ *Expect sexual temptation.* You already know it is part of life. So
accept that reality and keep in mind the important distinction between homosexual temptation and sin. Be prepared for temptation;
you cannot live in the world today and expect to totally avoid it. Each
morning pray that God will protect your mind as you go forth into
the world and face what's out there.

☐ *Identify your triggers to temptation.* Everyone has patterns of
temptation. Some are attacked with sexual thoughts upon waking up
or just prior to falling asleep. Others are susceptible when they are
tired late in the day or during times of stress.

There are seasonal factors. Men tend to struggle more in the
summer, when everyone dresses in skimpier clothing and the visual
stimulation soars. Others dread "family" holidays like Christmas or
Mother's Day, when feelings of loneliness can lead to overwhelming
sexual temptations. For women (and some men), temptation levels can
also follow a monthly cycle based on the body's hormonal changes.

TIME OUT

Begin taking a closer look at your own patterns. Write down your
sexual temptations for a period of several weeks (or even longer).
What time(s) of the day are the worst? What time(s) of the week? Of
the month? Of the year?

Many ex-gays have found help in taking a close look at their sexual
triggers. These sources of increased temptation can be physical (illness, tiredness, stress, pressure) or emotional (fear, anger, sadness,

humiliation, victimization, loneliness, emptiness, rejection, feeling overwhelmed).[1]

Triggers can also be spiritual in origin. Sometimes temptations come "from nowhere" with no emotional or physical stimulus you can identify. Temptations can arise from Satan, our enemy (see 2 Cor 11:3). But often these whispers from the enemy come in conjunction with some physical or emotional vulnerability. Jesus, for example, had been in the wilderness fasting for forty days when finally Satan appeared to him (Mt 4:2-3).

☐ *Develop preventive strategies.* Take control of your environment as much as you can. You cannot control the kind of magazines displayed at the local corner convenience store. But you can choose to go to a larger supermarket that does not sell pornography. Yes, it's a nuisance to stand in a checkout line, but what is more important? Your recovery process or waiting an extra few minutes? (You can use the time waiting in line to review your temptation patterns for that day!)

You also may not be able to control the fact that one of your co-workers, for example, is sexually attractive to you. But you can confess this attraction to a mature Christian friend or prayer partner, asking him or her to intercede for you and hold you accountable regarding this relationship. Some people find relief when they pray for the people they are attracted to, rather than fantasizing about them. I (Lori) shake off temptations to fantasize by recalling how bogged down I get spiritually when I indulge in vain imaginings. While fantasy yields some immediate pleasure, the consequences are oppressive and just not worth it.

Identifying Triggers: Emotional Needs and Temptation

I (Bob) realized the close relationship between homosexual temptation and emotions about a year after I had come to Love In Action. I was back home in Vancouver, Canada, driving to a Sunday evening church service. I became aware of my eyes being drawn to almost every man walking down the street as I drove by. My temptation level was noticeably higher than usual.

I did not have time to analyze the situation at the time, but later I thought about it. *What on earth was going on?* I asked myself. *What was I feeling at that moment?*

I realized I had been feeling nervous and insecure. That Sunday evening I had returned to my home church to share publicly my testimony of dealing with homosexuality in my life. These people had been my spiritual family for several years immediately prior to my move to California. I worried that they would reject me. I was feeling extremely vulnerable.

The evening service went well; none of my fears materialized. But the whole experience taught me an important lesson. *What am I feeling right now?* is an important question to ask when you are being tempted. What emotional needs are being expressed through the sexual temptation? Once the emotional need is identified, you can begin to find alternate ways to meet it.

Identifying Triggers: Fetishes and Partialisms

Most people have heard of fetishes, which are nonliving objects that become the source of sexual stimulation. Common examples are types of fabric (silk, leather), articles of clothing (underwear, shoes) or other objects which have become linked with sexual arousal. Fewer people have heard of *partialisms,* the term for nonsexual parts of the body that cause arousal (such as the nose, feet, biceps, mustache or legs).[2]

These patterns of sexual arousal are far more common in men than women, and they are very resistant to change. So do not be discouraged by lingering patterns from the past; the patterns of arousal will normally diminish over time. Make a conscious choice to resist such thoughts when they come to mind, without feeling condemned for having them. Also make a habit of praying against any spiritual influences which may be prompting them.

If you find yourself consistently nurturing memories of a past relationship, perhaps it is time to take some spiritual offensive action. With another person as your witness, verbally renounce the relationship, asking God's forgiveness for participating in sexual acts with that person. Ask God to sever the emotional and sexual ties formed in that relationship. And pray for that person's release from homosexuality or lesbianism.

Men, pray for insights into your particular partialisms. Realize that they are largely symbolic of your own needs and feelings of inadequacy. Specific parts of the body can represent what we are looking for—but lacking—in ourselves:

☐ *Arms.* Strength, protection, emotional stability (we feel vulnerable, unprotected)

☐ *Chest.* Father figure, maturity (we want nurturing, intimacy, closeness, affection, love)

☐ *Genitals.* Potency, manhood (we feel inadequate in our sense of masculinity)[3]

Women tend to be drawn to women with certain emotional qualities or personality types. However, physical characteristics can have a powerful pull for them too. Some women, particularly those who experienced a lack of nurturing from their mother, are drawn to women with large breasts. One former lesbian named Anna said, "When I meet a woman with big, soft brown eyes, I know I'm in trouble." Her first lover had large brown eyes, and this feature triggered Anna's attraction when she encountered it in other women.

Whatever we lack in ourselves, we are attracted to in other people. But having sex with others of our own gender will never increase our own masculinity or femininity. Homosexual relations are as effective as drinking salty water; both activities leave us unsatisfied, thirsting for more.

TIME OUT
Do you find yourself attracted to the same type of person over and over again? Ask God to show you the hidden dynamics to that attraction. For example, does that person resemble your first lover? Initial sexual experiences can powerfully influence future sexual attractions.

Identifying Triggers: Envy
Much same-sex lust is rooted in envy. We compare ourselves with others in terms of our physical makeup, emotional stability or spiritual maturity—and come up lacking. Then we begin to struggle with sexual attraction to them.

In talking to many people we have found common patterns to this struggle with envy. Usually our attractions fall into two categories:

☐ *Physical attributes.* We are short and we are attracted to someone tall; we are dark and we are attracted to someone fair; we are overweight and we are attracted to someone slender and athletic.

Some physical qualities are not changeable (for example, height). Uprooting envy involves accepting our unchangeable physical qualities, knowing that God planned every detail of our physical makeup (Ps 139:15-16).

Other physical qualities can be changed (for example, weight). If we are overweight and constantly drawn to the athletic type, we have to decide how much time and effort we are willing to put into our own physical fitness program.

□ *Personality.* We feel insecure and are attracted to someone confident; we are shy and attracted to the extrovert. Certain facts about our personality will never change substantially. If we are quiet, we may never be "the life of the party." But we can still mature and grow in our personality so that we have an inner confidence and strength that may be lacking right now.

"I've always been quiet," admits Brian. "I realize that I'll probably never be the entertainer, the clown at social gatherings. But that's OK with me now. I have become much more confident inside. I can speak up when I need to. And men with an outgoing personality, although still attractive to me, are no longer the source of envy and fantasy on my part."

Breaking Ties

Often our physical possessions can keep past associations alive in our emotions. One important aspect of making a break with our past is *cleansing our environment.* This principle includes the obvious symbols of our past: pornography, sex toys, gay or lesbian magazines and books, safe-sex posters.

But myriads of other possessions can provide strong emotional links with the past that we must prayerfully sort through:

□ *Mementos.* Souvenirs of special trips with a former lover; bracelets, watches or other significant gifts from gay friends; homosexual-related (especially seductive) photos, home movies, videotapes.

□ *Records, tapes, CDs.* Recordings by gay singers or pro-gay "folk" heroes, movies with gay themes, tapes that promote immorality or inappropriate sensuality, songs that were special to you and a certain gay friend or lover.

□ *Paperwork.* Membership cards and brochures from pro-gay churches and other organizations, discount cards to lesbian establishments, the little black book with phone numbers of former friends in the lifestyle, or "holy union" certificates.

□ *Clothing.* Invite the Holy Spirit (and perhaps also a counselor or discerning Christian friend) to show you the truth about your wardrobe. You can look for items such as outfits used to seduce others; apparel purchased because of its association with gay fashions; sexy underwear or lingerie that prompts wrong lustful feelings; leather jackets or pants that remind you of certain bars, people or immoral sexual practices.

When I (Lori) became a Christian, I had a favorite white blouse I had originally purchased to wear to bars or parties. Though it was relatively modest—not exactly something Madonna would want to borrow—I didn't feel comfortable wearing it anymore. In fact, I sensed the Holy Spirit prompting me to get rid of it. But it was new, and I liked it, so I decided to keep it. A few days later, my mom, finishing a load of laundry, apologetically displayed my special shirt: "Lori, somehow this blouse got washed with my new red towels." I took one look at it, mangled and covered with crimson splotches, and laughed. I should have listened to the Holy Spirit in the first place.

□ *Household goods and cars.* Sometimes even major possessions in your home or apartment must be given away or sold because of their strong association with a person or event you need to leave behind. One woman donated all her household furniture to a charitable organization when she moved out of the house she had shared with a longtime lover. Another man decided to sell his cherry-red sport convertible when he left the lifestyle. He had bought the car specifically to help him pick up other men while driving through the cruising areas in town.

"Delivered" of Homosexuality?

Do we ever find instant release from habitual behavior patterns? Many people look for quick solutions. Some ex-gay men and women have been deeply wounded by counselors who have tried to cast out "a spirit of homosexuality," presenting this deliverance as an instant solution to struggles with homosexuality. Later when the person experiences same-sex attractions, there can be great discouragement and overwhelming despair.

On the other hand, some former homosexuals are plagued by obsessive thoughts and habits that seem unaffected by the ordinary disciplines and strategies we discuss in this book. Some of these men and women have been involved in occult practices while in the gay lifestyle, including the use of "consciousness expanding" drugs. Others have engaged in heavy sadomasochistic rituals; still others have entered into sexual union with gay witches or warlocks. Any of these activities can potentially open a person to demonic oppression, which needs special attention from an experienced pastor or Christian counselor.

One woman tells about the differences that deliverance made in her life. Even after she had left her lesbian friends, she was plagued with nightmares and insistent "accusing voices" in her head, telling her she would never be free of lesbianism. She was also aware of "incredible emotional pain" that had always lurked within her. She felt overpowered by sexual temptations. She had also been involved in various occult-related activities.

In desperation she went for deliverance prayer. When her counselor began praying, her thoughts went berserk. "Stop! Stop her! Kill her!" the inner voices screamed. "Pick up the table and kill her." When the woman and her counselor began praying aloud against the demonic powers, she felt a relaxation occurring inside. In a five-hour follow-up session she verbally renounced spirits of homosexuality, anger, lust, witchcraft and many others.

When she walked out of the deliverance session, her spirit was soaring. She felt a dramatic difference inside and knew that God had set her free in a way she had never before experienced. Perhaps most important, however, was her realization that the deliverance was not the end of her struggles. "My new liberation did not obliterate the realization that what had taken place in those five hours represented just the surgery. A lifetime of choices—difficult choices to walk in obedience to God's Spirit—lay ahead." Deliverance can give a fresh start, but it is not an instant cure.

So far in this chapter we have talked about general principles of temptation. Now let's apply these insights to several common problems.

Masturbation

"Is masturbation a sin?" is usually the first question discussed in most books which address this topic. Everyone has differing opinions; however, most do agree on one thing: the Bible is silent about the practice of masturbation.[4]

Here is a more relevant question to ask at this point: "How is masturbation affecting my recovery process?" Is it pushing you forward into new levels of freedom—or dragging you back into old thought patterns?

Most ex-gays and former lesbians find masturbation a negative influence on their healing process because it is accompanied by lesbian or gay fantasies. Obviously, as long as such memories or fantasies are reinforced, we will not make much progress in moving away from a homosexual mindset.

For many, masturbation is also an addiction. In biblical terms we have become "slaves to sin" (Rom 6:6). We no longer have control over the practice. Our sexuality rules us, rather than us having control of our sexual appetite.

Some men and women have found that the guilt and separation from God they sense after masturbating opens them up to spiritual warfare on other issues. This habit can trigger temptation in other, more overt, areas of sexual sin.

Masturbation can be compared to binging on junk food. It satisfies the physical appetite for the moment but often leaves you feeling sick and empty. That is because God created sex to be more than a release of tension. He wants it to promote love, commitment and permanence in a marriage relationship. Masturbation lacks any of these qualities.

We have found that most ex-gays want to stop this practice. Why is it so hard to overcome? Because there are so many complex motivations which prompt this behavior pattern.

☐ *Physical motivations.* Men have a continual production of semen, which is stored in two internal "storage tanks" called the seminal vesicles. When these are filled, the sexual drive comes alive and the desire for some sort of release becomes conscious. So the desire for a sexual release can arise strongly in a man's mind without any sinful encouragement on his part.

With women there are also difficulties. At certain times in the monthly cycle higher levels of hormones (androgens and possibly estrogens) raise a woman's sexual desires, increasing the temptation to masturbate. Getting through these days can be extremely difficult for many women.

Do these physical facts mean that masturbation is unavoidable? No. But they explain, in part, why masturbation is such a common struggle.

☐ *Emotional motivations.* Masturbation is also linked to our emotional needs. If you doubt this, notice when your desire to masturbate is strongest. Typically, the struggle intensifies when you are experiencing certain emotions, such as loneliness, fear, anger or boredom. Masturbation does nothing to help resolve these feelings.

Steps Out

Most of us want to overcome masturbation. What steps can we take to accomplish this goal?[5]

☐ *Make no provision for the flesh.* Sometimes we need to be practical in fighting sin. We can set ourselves up for temptation without even realizing it.

Larry realized that he always masturbated after shaving in the morning. Following his shower he would stand in front of the mirror, naked, when the temptation would hit. Other men have discovered a similar pattern. Most guys are visually stimulated by nudity—even their own. Larry found that his temptations lessened when he took the simple step of putting on a bathrobe before shaving.

Others are commonly tempted just as they are drifting off to sleep. If this is your weakness, begin taking note of what you have been reading or seeing on television just before bedtime. Has the input been less than profitable? Consider possible alternate activities: a short devotional time or listening to worshipful tapes before turning out the light.

☐ *Look for emotional roots.* When you sense the desire to masturbate, ask yourself, *What am I feeling right now?* Are you feeling lonely? Bored? Tired? Angry? Frustrated? Anxious? Depressed?

Any of these emotions can become a trigger for the temptation. But a physical release will not meet the underlying emotional need. Once you have identified the emotions you are experiencing, begin seeking God for practical wisdom on how to better meet that need.

Perhaps one evening you are lonely. So you have to take the initiative to reach out to someone, like calling a friend from work or writing to an old friend from your college youth group. If you need comfort, maybe you need to take the evening off, wrap up in your favorite blanket with a cup of hot chocolate and enjoy a favorite old movie.

These are just examples of how we can begin to meet our legitimate needs in appropriate ways, rather than masturbating to temporarily numb our feelings. We have to be willing to feel—and seek resolution for—the underlying emotional pain prompting the escape into masturbation.

☐ *Seek accountability.* Problems like masturbation thrive in secrecy. When the problem is brought into the light and shared with another person, there is new power to overcome it.

"Confess your faults to one another" and "Walk in the light" are two common exhortations (Jas 5:16 and 1 Jn 1:7). Unfortunately, too few Christians are willing to open up this private area of their lives to others. But masturbation is almost a universal struggle among singles, particularly men. So this is an ideal area for mutual accountability among Christians—and it does not necessarily mean the confession of homosexual struggles if you are not yet that open with fellow believers.

☐ *Put the issue in perspective.* Almost all singles (and many marrieds) have struggled with masturbation. So you are not unique, a bad person or a spiritual basket case. You are simply an average person with a common struggle.

Be realistic. If you have been indulging in this behavior for years, don't expect that the temptation will vanish overnight. It is going to take consistent effort and emotional maturity to overcome. If your habit is decreasing in frequency, that's great! Be encouraged that you are making progress. And ask God to give you an increased desire to please him in *all* areas of your life.

Pornography

The temptation toward pornography is a common struggle, especially among ex-gay men. Often it is used to replace flesh-and-blood relationships. Pornography can become an obsession, giving a physical high much like drugs or alcohol.[6]

An important step in gaining victory, as with masturbation and other sex-related habits, is to identify your triggers and develop prevention strategies. The same strategies that you use to break the masturbation habit will work for pornography too. Confession to a mature friend or church leader is *essential.* For married men or women, your confidant should be your spouse. Graphic details are unnecessary, but the promise to confess all future episodes of pornographic consumption will give you an increased level of resistance when temptation suddenly hits you.

Of course, you must terminate your subscriptions to gay publications, which feed your sexual lusts. You do not need to know the latest tidbits about the homosexual and lesbian subculture. These days most newspapers of large cities contain enough news about the gay community to keep you more than informed about significant developments.

If you can't stop glancing through forbidden magazines when you stop at the corner market, make a deliberate choice to avoid patronizing stores which sell them. If you like reading news magazines, take out a subscription for home delivery, or visit your local library, which probably has an excellent selection of current periodicals. If you are willing to work at it, you *can* find freedom, although you may have to fight long and hard to win the battle.

Anonymous Sex
For many gay men the majority of their sexual experiences have been with other men who were strangers or casual acquaintances. "At first I dreamed about a long-term relationship," confesses Byron. "But after a few lover relationships fell apart, I gave up hope. After that, I was happy just to connect sexually with another man for an evening."

Casual sex can bring physical pleasure and temporary fulfillment. But often, in the long run, a series of anonymous encounters leaves a person feeling used and depressed. You wonder, *Does anyone love me for anything more than my body?* And, as the years pass, it becomes increasingly difficult to find such liaisons with desirable men.

We believe that casual sex, at its root, is a flight from emotional intimacy. A one-night stand is a pseudointimacy which gives a false sense of being close to another person. But it is one-dimensional—purely physical—without the deep emotional and relational dynamics that God intended as the context for human sexual fulfillment.

To break out of this behavior pattern, we must be willing to forsake this pattern of false intimacy and begin investing in true intimacy.

We must let down our façades and let our Christian friends see the real person. For some of us this is a huge step of faith to take.

"I spent all my life pretending that I had it all together," Byron says. "I was terrified to let people know the 'real me.' What if they didn't like who I really was inside?"

Many people addicted to casual sex have a severe struggle with self-esteem; they hold such a low view of themselves that they sincerely believe no one would like them if their real character flaws were known. Rather than taking the risk of stepping out into the light of honest relationships, they spend their whole lives chasing alluring shadows. They end up in darkness, alone and unfulfilled.

If you have been addicted to casual sex, the only way out is to take the risk—to come out from behind your walls of pseudoperfection and let people know the real person that God has created you to be. Many ex-gays who have taken this risk have found their efforts richly rewarded.

"I never really opened up to others until about two years ago," Byron explains. "It was terrifying—but I knew that it was the only way to escape my depressive sense of isolation. I've been surprised at the results. Now I can hardly remember how lonely my life was. I've found several genuine friends, and we're able to express our love and affection for each other in healthy ways. Although I still occasionally feel a pull toward a one-night stand, I've found that those kinds of temptations are getting less and less in my life. I'm really excited about how far the Lord has brought me."

7

WHAT'S ON YOUR MIND?

*W*ill *you successfully overcome homosexuality? The answer to* that question depends on what happens in your mind. Your thought life is the battlefield where victory is really won or lost.

Some attempts to overcome sexual temptation—cold showers to avoid masturbation, changing jobs to escape an attractive coworker, moving to a new apartment to avoid a gay neighbor—may be only temporary solutions. If the underlying reasons for being homosexually tempted are not discovered and resolved, these solutions are like putting a cork into the spout of a dripping tap. The water pressure continues to build, and at some point the cork blows off and the water comes rushing out. A better solution is to turn off the water at its source. Similarly, we must get to the source of our continuing temptations to be freed of them.

The Inner Battleground

Winning the war of your thought life will be one of your toughest challenges as a Christian. You may have experienced defeat for so long in this area that you wonder if victory is even possible.

In Romans 12:2 Paul commands us, "Do not conform any longer to the pattern of this world, but be transformed by the renewing of your mind." Applying his words to our situation means that to break with the mindset and actions of the homosexual lifestyle, we must change our thinking.

Ex-gay men and women have to fight this battle on three main fronts:

☐ *Memories of the past.* It is not unusual for an ex-gay man to have had dozens, if not hundreds, of past sexual encounters. Other ex-gay men and former lesbians have had long-term relationships; a few have had no overt sexual experiences but may have indulged in homosexual-related activities, such as pornographic magazines and movies. But whether our homosexual experiences have been extensive or limited, we all have memories of the past to overcome.

☐ *Sexual fantasies.* Our imagination is an incredible gift from God with potential for tremendous good or evil. Immoral fantasies can be especially troubling to those of us with little overt homosexual experiences who have spent years escaping into daydreams of imaginary erotic and romantic same-sex relationships.

☐ *Distorted patterns of thought.* There are also nonsexual areas where we can struggle in our mind, such as thoughts about our relationship with God *(God hates me because I'm gay),* thoughts about our relationships with other people *(I'll never be able to relate to other women)* and thoughts about our future *(I'll always be gay).* Unless these thought patterns change, we will be continually defeated and discouraged in our recovery process.

Fantasies

Often we gauge someone's success in overcoming homosexuality by how he or she acts in public. A more accurate gauge of freedom is what takes place when our mind is idle. Where do our fantasies take us then?

All of us are going to have thoughts enter our minds that are ungodly. When this occurs, we have three options: indulgence, repression or replacement.[1] Obviously, to indulge in homosexual fantasies is sinful. That means we have two other reasonable options:

☐ *Repression.* Many Christian books suggest various techniques to conquer lust that, at first reading, sound very spiritual. Here is a common one: When you are tempted to fantasize impure thoughts, quote an appropriate Bible verse.

This type of strategy is effective for the moment, but "repression" techniques are not a long-term solution. To conquer ingrained thought patterns, you have to deal with the underlying emotional and spiritual needs feeding them.

We are *not* trying to minimize the importance of knowing God's Word. However, we have talked to many people who were told to "just pray more" or "quote a verse when you are tempted." Their counselors did not take them any deeper, and these persons eventually returned to homosexual activities in discouragement, because their temptations did not diminish over time.

Now let's compare that solution with a more effective answer:

□ *Replacement.* The lies of our past must be replaced with the truths of God's Word. Reading the Bible is essential but not just so we can repeat a verse as a "magic mantra" in the midst of temptation. Rather, through the diligent, regular study and *application* of biblical principles, we experience changes in the way we look at God, the world and ourselves.

Our worldview evolves into an outlook that reflects the truth, rather than the distortions of our secular society. We come to discover the reality of God's love for us as individuals (see Rom 5:8) and his desire to forgive us for all sin—including homosexual thoughts and actions (1 Jn 1:9). The Bible's perspective, when acted upon in our daily lives, will profoundly change the way we see our past and chart our future.

Dealing with Memories

Our memory is a marvelous gift, but it can also seem like a curse at times. If we previously indulged in sexual sin, it is hard to forget graphic details. "This was a major problem for me," Cheryl said. "I'd reflect on the great times: the excitement when my lover and I first met, camping trips we took together, parties with other friends from the lifestyle. All too often, I'd forget the bitter fights we had, the jealous power plays when I worried she was attracted to someone else."

Cheryl's words provide an important insight: memories are rarely accurate in every detail. They get twisted with time. Unfortunately, often we magnify the good times in the past, the fun we had in homosexual activities, the excitement, glamour and sexual thrills. But we forget the nights of loneliness, the frustrations of seeking a long-term relationship, the anguish of being left for another lover, the fear of sexually transmitted diseases, the depression of knowing your family disapproves of your relationships.

When you are plagued by old memories, ask God to give you a true, full picture of the past, especially when you find yourself only remembering the positive aspects. Memories *do* fade with time. We can hasten their demise by not dwelling on them or reinforcing them.

TIME OUT
Periodically it is helpful to review the reasons you decided to leave homosexuality in the first place. Write down your reasons, and add to the list in weeks to come as further reasons come to mind.

Other Practical Tips
Problems with inappropriate thoughts can occur at certain times of the day, such as upon awakening or just before going to sleep. Problems can also occur when our mind enters "neutral," such as when we are driving a familiar route to work or performing repetitious tasks at work. I (Bob) have found it helpful to install a cassette player in my car, and I constantly have sermons, lectures or music tapes playing to keep my mind occupied while I drive. At other times I record favorite Christian radio programs, which I can replay during my commute to work and back home. An increasing number of excellent books are also available on tape.

Some thought patterns are simply bad habits from the past; others are based on past associations. For example, if you and your gay friends always attended a drag event at Halloween, it will be natural for you to associate that evening with past times. If birthdays were celebrated with wild partying and sex, those memories may be triggered each year for a while. It will take time to develop different annual patterns; be patient with yourself while new associations and memories are built up in your mind. Plan ahead, so you can have fun activities scheduled for those anniversaries and other difficult times when memories will arise from the past.

Never Acted Out

For those men and women who have never acted out their homosexual feelings with another person, the mind is the main area of the battle.[2] If you are in this situation, I (Bob) can relate. Even though I went through my teens and twenties with strong homosexual feelings, I was a virgin when I married at age thirty-four. I avoided the sexual experimentation of many teens and young adults. I was also naive about homosexuality. I grew up in the era before "gay rights" became so open; I didn't know about the gay bars in my city until after I went to college.

But from an early age I was mindful of the eternal consequences of my day-to-day choices. I knew that someday God would require an account of my earthly actions: "For we must all appear before the judgment seat of Christ, that each one may receive what is due him for the things done while in the body, whether good or bad" (2 Cor 5:10). That knowledge kept me from outwardly falling into homosexual relationships (although it did not keep me from sinful fantasies).

The person who has not acted on his or her homosexual feelings faces some unique struggles:

☐ *Trivialization by others.* I have found that some people tend to minimize my past struggles with homosexuality. "Oh, you weren't really gay," they say. "Wait until you hear what I've been through!" Their comments make me feel judged, as if my struggles have been minimal. For all they know, my temptations may actually have been stronger than their own but I had the self-control (and God's grace) to remain abstinent.

☐ *Added identity confusion.* The homosexual man or woman with no sexual experiences can have many internal questions: *If I have not had any homosexual experiences, does that mean I never was really gay? How do my temptations differ from other ex-gays'?* This kind of inner confusion can lead to ambivalence about needing or seeking help.

☐ *Identity isolation.* Men and women with homosexual or lesbian feelings who have never acted on them can really feel isolated from everyone—ex-gay or straight! These feelings can be accentuated when the person visits an ex-gay support group and hears other members making reference to their past sexual experiences and relationships.

Some of these men and women have never been inside a gay bar or read a homosexual magazine. Some have never talked to another person struggling with inappropriate same-sex attractions. They do not know the current gay "lingo"; they wonder what the gay lifestyle is really like. These feelings of alienation can lead to temptations to break down the boundaries of their innocence: *Just one time won't hurt anybody,* they think, or, *If I have a sexual experience, I'll get it out of my system.*

☐ *Increased homosexual temptations.* Temptations are often triggered by feelings of isolation, as well as rejection from others. Knowing you are different from the "average" Christian overcoming homosexuality can trigger even more sexual temptation. So, contrary to what some people might think, men and women who have never acted out can have *stronger* homosexual temptations because of their relative innocence (they have not yet experienced the negative side of physical involvement).

They battle against the curiosity factor *(I wonder what it would be like to . . .).* People who have had gay relationships can look back at both good and bad experiences, so their view of homosexuality is probably more realistic.

Fortunately, I (Bob) never struggled much with feelings of being different from the other guys when I joined the Love In Action ministry. All of us had some differences in our backgrounds, so I focused on what I had in common with others and worked on forming the supportive friendships that I desperately needed.

Later I realized that my struggles were similar to those of ex-gay men who have been celibate for several years. We were dealing with the same root issues, similar emotional struggles and the same daily choices to follow God. Our similarities far outnumbered our differences.

One last word for the man or woman who has never acted out: Sexual virginity is scorned in today's society. It is treated as an embarrassment, rather than an admirable trait. But remember that your sexual purity is a special gift that you can give away only one time. Do not allow other people to convince you that it is not worth much. I'm glad that I didn't.

Secondary Virginity

Whether or not we have been sexually active in the past, however, God delights to give us a new beginning. We can be washed and purified by him, so that we become "virgins" in his eyes. He will help us overcome memories of our unrighteous past. He actually forgets our sexual sins: "I, even I, am he who blots out your transgressions, for my own sake, and remembers your [sexual] sins no more" (Is 43:25).

Some people have referred to this regained state of innocence as *secondary virginity*. It is a precious gift from a loving God—available to any former homosexual who wants it.

Reality of Spiritual Warfare

The idea that the devil is a personal being who can influence our lives is dismissed with a laugh by much of our society. But the Scriptures teach that Satan is a fallen angel of great power with direct access to our lives. "Your enemy the devil prowls around like a roaring lion looking for someone to devour" (1 Pet 5:8). He is identified as a tempter "who leads the whole world astray" (1 Thess 3:5; Rev 12:9). We can make two mistakes in dealing with Satan: living in excessive fear, or ignoring his existence altogether.

God gives us divine protection against the enemy. You have probably heard sermons on the spiritual armor of Ephesians chapter six, but have you ever applied these pieces of armor to your battle against homosexuality? Here are some examples:

□ *Belt of truth.* Principle: God's Word—and not my own feelings—determine what is true.

Applications: God loves me, even though I struggle with homosexual feelings and behavior: "But God demonstrates his own love for us in this: While we still were sinners, Christ died for us" (Rom 5:8). God is able to help me not stumble back into homosexual behavior: "To him who is able to keep you from falling" (Jude 24). God stands with me in my fight against gay or lesbian sin: "If God be for us, who can be against us?" (Rom 8:31 KJV).

□ *Breastplate of righteousness.* Principle: My impure heart is cleansed by the blood of Christ.

Applications: When I repent, Jesus cleanses me from all homosexual sin, including lustful thoughts, masturbation or sexual encounters: "the blood of Jesus, his Son, purifies us from all sin" (1 Jn 1:7). Despite my ongoing homosexual temptations, I can be righteous in Christ, "not having a righteousness of my own that comes from the law, but that which is through faith in Christ" (Phil 3:9).

TIME OUT
Look up Ephesians 6:10-18 and list the other parts of your spiritual armor. Make specific applications to your battle against homosexuality.

Rebuilding the Wall

I (Bob) like to compare our mind to a walled city of Old Testament times. The thick, high barrier protects the inhabitants by keeping enemies out. But when we have indulged in sexual fantasies for many years, our mind is like a city with the wall broken down. The stones are lying scattered on the ground. Our spiritual enemies—Satan and his demonic hosts—have free access to our minds. They can run in and out at will.

We have to rebuild the walls of our mind, erecting a spiritual barrier of purity and strength against the invasion of these enemies and their temptations of impure, lustful thoughts. The wall is not built up again overnight; it has been broken down over a long period. It will take some consistent, long-term effort to restore the wall.

There are many ways to rebuild the wall, besides the basics of Bible reading, prayer and church attendance. Each time we engage in these activities and choose to think pure, godly thoughts, we put another "brick" in place on the wall. Here are some practical suggestions for your own rebuilding program:

□ *Watch interesting, upbuilding videos,* including contemporary films, concerts, nature films (such as "Sermons from Science"), Bible teaching and lectures on recovery from homosexuality and other relevant topics (see appendix C).

□ *Read Christian books and magazines,* especially those that focus on your interests (for example, women's issues, men's testimonies, sports profiles, contemporary Christian music, marriage and family). And don't forget Christian classics by authors such as C. S. Lewis, George MacDonald, Charles Williams and John Bunyan.

□ *Listen to uplifting Christian music tapes or compact discs,* which are available in every style, ranging from pop to country to classical to rock. Some tapes feature Scriptures set to music, an excellent way to absorb God's Word and its principles.

☐ *Spend time with godly friends* in a wide variety of settings, from formal Bible studies to fun times over pizza. Even when your conversation is not about spiritual matters, the fact that these friends share your love for God helps reinforce your biblical perspective.

☐ *Don't dismiss classic secular books and movies* that reflect the biblical foundations of our culture. Often they focus on faith, sacrifice, commitment and other wholesome values that support a godly worldview. Input does not have to be strictly limited to religious books, music, movies and magazines to help us reinforce the truths of Scripture.

Just as our old mindset of homosexuality was tentative at first, then reinforced repeatedly by our thoughts and activities, so our Christian mindset must be developed slowly and consistently over a long period of time. The Bible refers to this process as "renewing the mind" (see Rom 12:2), which is one of the most important principles of attaining significant freedom from gay or lesbian thoughts and feelings.

Getting Proper Support

Often, deep-rooted issues in our lives are more than we can deal with alone. Before coming to Love In Action, I (Bob) found a certain amount of resolution regarding some root issues in my life (the roots that we discussed back in chapter four). But, as certain temptation patterns continued, I sensed a need for something more in terms of specialized help.

Perhaps you have found many new insights through this book, but now you are beginning to realize that you need additional support. What are your options?

☐ *Accountability partner.* Many men and women who are not living near a specialized ministry find support through being accountable to one person regarding their sexual struggles. This person may be a pastor, elder or mature friend in Christ. Sometimes such accountability can arise from deep friendships developed within a church or Bible study group. We do *not* recommend that you form such a relationship with another ex-gay, especially if there are sexual or emotional attractions between you. Perhaps a married couple is available to you. Pray for God's leading in this important matter.

☐ *Covenant group.* This is a small prayer and sharing group of four or five individuals who are mutually accountable. I (Bob) have found much encouragement through my involvement in this type of group with three other married Christian men. Perhaps your church would be interested in starting such a group if none exists.

☐ *Professional counseling.* We have known numerous former homosexuals who have found tremendous benefit from a season of one-on-one counseling with a trained Christian professional. Check the yellow pages of a phone directory in your city or the nearest large town. A few phone calls to the largest churches in your county may also give you some leads on potential counselors. Be sure to ascertain where a counselor stands on the basic issues of Christianity, as well as his or her position on homosexuality. We feel it is important that a counselor share your convictions regarding the biblical view of homosexuality.

☐ *Ministry of healing prayer.* Some deep-rooted issues seem unmovable, even though you have sought counseling and long-term accountability. There may be help for you through healing prayer, sometimes referred to as "inner healing" or "healing of memories." This specialized ministry, under the direction of the Holy Spirit, can expose early life experiences that left us vulnerable to homosexuality and other problems. This prayer does not change our early experiences, but it allows us to gain a new perspective on these experiences, which eliminates their power over us.

☐ *Support group meetings.* Dozens of ex-gay support groups exist that have been helpful to thousands of participants. For a list of groups, contact Exodus International (see appendix C). If no such group exists in your area, other groups (Homosexuals Anonymous, groups for overcoming sexual addiction, etc.) may give you local accountability and peer support.

☐ *In-depth counseling program.* Several ex-gay ministries have live-in discipleship programs, where individuals live together in houses and go through a lengthy program (perhaps for a one-year period). Other ministries have programs that, although not residential, require a commitment for a certain time (such as six or nine months of attending weekly meetings). Many men and women have found tremendous benefit from being involved in these more intensive programs. A list of such programs is available through Exodus International.

8

CHANGE IN SELF-IDENTITY

*W*e live in an age where almost everyone feels entitled to at least one identity crisis. The big question, Who am I? can come upon us at any time: teen years, college graduation, the onset of parenthood and, of course, midlife. We all have done some soul-searching on this subject, but probably few are more likely to encounter an identity crisis than gay men or lesbian women who become Christians.

"Am I gay or am I Christian? Can I even be homosexual and Christian at the same time? If being a Christian means I am no longer homosexual, then what am I? I am definitely *not* straight!"

Men and women who are into homosexuality react intensely to the idea of giving up the gay or lesbian label: "No one is going to push me back into the closet." Members of the pro-gay church movement might add the lie, "God made me this way. Why should I change?"

If pressed further on the issue of changing their identity, gays will probably acknowledge a second reaction—puzzlement. "How could I even think of giving up something that is so much a part of me? If I did, what would be left?"

Counting the Cost

Why do homosexuals fight so hard for their lesbian or gay identity? Because they invested enormously in accepting that identity in the first place.

For many the first awareness of homosexual desires came around the time of puberty.[1] Initial feelings of excitement and curiosity quickly gave way to confusion, shame and despair. Then came a period of struggling to appear "normal": trying to bury same-sex desires, exaggerating or fabricating heterosexual interest, wrestling with guilt and fear of discovery.

After a time of internal pain and struggle, many feel relief and exhilaration in finally proclaiming "I am gay." Some eagerly explore all that the lifestyle has to offer: new friends, values and politics. They embrace a completely different way of looking at the world and, especially, a new way of looking at themselves.

Let's say this has been your experience. Now you have come to Christ or rededicated your life to him. Before long—maybe immediately—you know God's Word does not condone homosexual or lesbian activity. No matter how many times you read Romans 1, looking for loopholes, you know homosexual acts are wrong. So you stop having homosexual sex or at least attempt to stop.

Identity Versus Behavior

"But what's wrong with having a homosexual identity?" you might ask. "If I'm not acting out homosexually, do I really need to give up the gay identity?"

Difficult as it may seem, the answer is yes. The healing and transformation God wants to do is thorough—from the inside out. Here are two reasons why our old identity must be released:

☐ *The homosexual identity is based on our sinful past.* As believers in Jesus, all of us are commanded to put aside our old identity, whether that be homosexual, drug-user, or yuppie golf addict. We are called to embrace a new lifestyle in Christ Jesus. "Put off your old self, which is being corrupted by its deceitful desires . . . [and] put on the new self," Paul exhorts in Ephesians 4:22-24.

☐ *The homosexual identity is based on our present temptations.* We may still be tempted homosexually, but that does not make us gay or lesbian. Our identity in Christ is not defined by the things that tempt us.

As Hebrews 4:15 reminds us, Jesus was "tempted in every way just as we are—yet was without sin." There is a clear inference here that Jesus was tempted sexually. Yet his identity never became "Jesus the fornicator" or "Jesus the adulterer." No matter how he was tempted, he remained the sinless Son of God. We, of course, are not sinless. But neither are we defined by our temptations.

Our identity is not found by looking backward to our past or by looking inward to our fleshly nature. Both of these indicators will give us a false report about who we are. To find our true identity, we must look elsewhere.

The Search for Identity

"You are heterosexual in Christ," the speaker said and I (Bob) shifted uncomfortably in my seat. "No matter how deep your homosexual feelings are, deeper still lies your heterosexuality, buried under a thousand fears."

I will never forget that lecture by Colin Cook at the 1982 Exodus International conference in Denver, an annual event for leaders in ex-gay ministry. By this time I had been part of a ministry to homosexuals in California for over three years. Yet I felt shaken deep inside with a queasy feeling I couldn't identify.

Am I really heterosexual? I wondered in the following weeks. How could I honestly claim to have a heterosexual identity? I did not feel heterosexual. I was not sexually attracted to women. I still had homosexual feelings for other men.

In some ways I felt trapped in a "no-man's land" of sexuality: no longer claiming a homosexual identity, yet feeling foreign to the idea of a heterosexual identity.

Did God expect me to "fake it" in terms of my feelings? Should I somehow "step out in faith" and believe I was heterosexual, especially for the sake of a strong public testimony to the media and those I ministered to?

Over the years I have moved into a new perspective on this question. As I look into God's Word, I realize that all the basics I need to know about who I am are right before me.

Genesis 1:27 is a good starting place: "So God created man in his own image, in the image of God he created him; male and female he created them."

First, I see that each of us is created "in his own image." Being created in the image of God is something to ponder. This side of eternity, we will never begin to comprehend all that this means.

In making us after his image, God has invested us with immeasurable value. On a good day I may see myself as Bob Davies—a nice, competent, heterosexual man. On a bad day I see Bob Davies as frustrated, struggling, someone who will never measure up. But when God looks at me, he sees Bob Davies—made in his own image, planned from all eternity, a marvel!

Our backgrounds, our hurts, even our bathroom mirror may tell us we are worthless creatures, powerless to change. But God's Word tells us we are made in his image, implying we have abilities, privileges and responsibilities far beyond anything we have let ourselves imagine. Each of us, regardless of our limitations, is much more valuable—and much more capable—than we think.

The Genesis account goes on, without even beginning a new sentence, to give us the next solid building block for our identity: "male and female he created them."

Here again there is not much room for speculation. We have male and we have female. Both are created in God's image. Each reflects a unique dimension of God's character. Each has much to tell us about who God is, what he is like.

Notice that there are only two categories. Either we are a man made in God's image or a woman made in God's image. No third option is mentioned.

We believe the Fall (Gen 3) marked the beginning of all sexual twistedness, including homosexuality. But as disfiguring as sin is, it does not change our deepest identity in God. Each of us, no matter how afflicted, is still created in God's image, created male or female, possessing the full potential for all these words imply.

TIME OUT

The Bible never speaks of homosexuality as a person's identity but simply condemns homosexual *actions*. The labels "homosexual" and "heterosexual" have no biblical precedent. For example, the Greek word *arsenokoitai,* translated as "homosexual" in some modern versions (1 Cor 6:9 RSV), means literally "a man who lies [sexually] with another man."

The Bible distinguishes behavior from identity. What is the implication for those who have taken "gay" or "lesbian" as their identity?

Detachment from Our Own Gender

In childhood Russell felt strangely detached from other boys. "I always felt like I was on the outside, looking at men as if they were behind glass, like museum specimens. There was no emotional connection with other boys or men, just a longing for them as I grew older that I didn't really understand."

This feeling of separation from one's own sex can also occur in women. Former lesbian Jeanette Howard says she used to feel more like a "third sex" than male or female. "For years I was a gender-identity itinerant, migrating somewhere between the masculine, feminine and neuter," she recalls in her book, *Out of Egypt.*[2]

A major turning point came in Jeanette's life after she had been a Christian for two years. A teacher at her Bible school challenged her to stand in front of the mirror every morning and thank God that he had made her a woman. She thought it sounded like a ridiculous task, but she tried to follow this suggestion.

"The next morning," she says, "I got up and struggled to look at myself in the mirror. Try as I would, I could not acknowledge myself as truly female.

"Day after day I persevered. For the first week I fought merely to hold my gaze at the mirror, unable to utter a word. After about ten days, I was able to look at myself full face. But when it came to saying anything, I could not speak. I just cried, too frightened to acknowledge who I was."

Finally, after several weeks, Jeanette was able to stand in front of the mirror and say, "Thank you, Father, for making me a woman." Although the acknowledgment came only with great difficulty, Jeanette says this was a key step for her to take in the process of changing her gender identification.

"Coming into agreement with God . . . meant acknowledging that he not only knew me but approved of me," Jeanette said. "He chose me to be a woman. In fact, he saw me as being completely female, irrespective of my own thoughts on the matter."

No longer would Jeanette refer to herself as a Christian "person," as she had for several years. "From now on," she said, "out of obedience to God, I would call myself a Christian *woman*."[3]

Embracing Our Gender Identity

Many men and women dealing with homosexual issues feel ambivalent or even hostile to embracing their gender identity. They may feel "cheated" out of the excitement, challenges, or comfort that they perceive is inherent to being a member of the opposite sex. Others affirm the gender they were born with but feel detached from—or even repulsed by—many of the traits and qualities generally associated with that gender. Coming to terms with our gender means acknowledging the scriptural perspective on our true sexual identity:

□ *God planned our gender before we were even conceived.* "Before I formed you in the womb I knew you, before you were born I set you apart," God said to Jeremiah (Jer 1:5). Our gender is not an accident; it is a vital part of our personhood that is planned by God.

□ *God assigned our gender to fulfill specific purposes through us.* The psalmist said, "Your eyes saw my unformed body. All the days ordained for me were written in your book before one of them came to be" (Ps 139:16).

God had a specific purpose in creating us as male or female. The call that he placed on our life is best accomplished through the gender he has given us. There are numerous scriptural illustrations of this principle: Mary's ability to bear children enabled her to "be with child through the Holy Spirit" (Mt 1:18), and Moses' upbringing in Pharaoh's household resulted from his male gender (Ex 1:16; 2:2-10). God has sovereign reasons for creating us as male or female.

Developing Masculinity/Femininity: Embracing God's Choice

Our past lack of acceptance—real acceptance—of our gender identity has resulted in an immaturity in our self-concept as a man or woman.[4] "Part of me still feels like a little boy" may be an adult man's true inner feelings. "I'm just coming to realize that I am a woman" is a surprising discovery for an adult female.

How can we grow in our sexual identity? How can we encourage that part of ourself, the part traditionally labeled "masculine" or "feminine," which is still underdeveloped?

The maturing process begins with the decision to *embrace our masculinity or femininity,* even if we are scared to death of the implications.

Often we have rejected God's plan for us as men and women. Women have used the lesbian lifestyle as a protective shield, shutting out men—who often represent pain and abuse. Men have embraced the fantasy of homosexuality as an escape from male responsibility and mature relationships with women. Now we must face our fears and, with God's help, walk through them.

"Jesus, show me what it means to be a woman. Take away my fears about whether I belong or can fit into the expectations of others. Show me who you want me to be."

"Lord, I thank you for making me a man. I'm willing to grow in my masculinity, so show me how to take the next step. Give me the courage I need to relate honestly to other men. With your help I'm willing to face my fears."

Repenting of Wrong Attitudes

☐ *Women.* For many women in the lesbian lifestyle, *being in control* is more than just a desirable attribute. It is a guiding life principle. As we saw in chapter four, many lesbians have been victims of sexual and emotional abuse and have vowed in response, "No one is ever going to hurt me like that again. I am going to call the shots from now on."

Qualities that are often labeled "feminine"—such as being open, yielded, trusting—are pushed into the background, especially in relationship to men. Other qualities, ones that our culture traditionally associates with masculinity, are cultivated: aggressiveness, quick decision-making, "toughness," independence. For the ex-lesbian, the idea of being open and trusting in her responses might be enough to send her running out of the church, back to the comfort and familiarity of the lesbian lifestyle.

Often ex-lesbians fear that "healing" implies that they will be forced into getting married and having children, a prospect that may sound as appealing as a lifetime prison sentence.

I (Lori) can understand this fear. While growing up, I lacked confidence that I was a "real woman." I didn't think I was pretty, and flirting with boys never came naturally to me. Even after I became a Christian, I felt more neutral than feminine.

One warm Saturday afternoon, our church held a fellowship lunch for women at a local park. I was single, not even dating at the time, and it seemed the whole park was filled with young mothers cooing over their newborn babies. I found these women hard to relate to, and the whole scene revolted me. These women seemed to ooze femininity and maternal contentment. I wanted no part of it and, yet, I was jealous.

Twelve years, marriage, and three children later, my views have changed. I love being a mother. But accepting and embracing the many aspects of femaleness has been, and still is, an ongoing process.

When an ex-gay woman comes to Christ, she has already taken a major step toward reclaiming her identity as a woman. She has opened up her life to a man—Jesus! As he begins to heal her hurts, as she faces past rejection and abuse, acknowledging pain, anguish and violation, she begins to experience Jesus' empathy and love. His healing and forgiveness begin flowing in her life.

While she starts realizing the need to trust God and let go of control, old fears jump up to stare her in the face: "What if I get hurt again?" Feelings she has not been in touch with for years begin to surface—childhood memories of vulnerability, sorrow, a desire to be loved and protected. This all can be so frightening that she retreats back into her "in control" position.

One of the most healing aspects of coming to Christ and beginning to trust him is that bit by bit, we are freed from the driving motivation to protect ourselves. We realize that our Father is a faithful and strong nurturer. He will protect us from harm as he gently leads us into deeper and deeper healing.

Though some—actually, many—of the revelations we have about ourselves are painful, his love and comfort are there to offset our insecurities. In time, our consuming desire for control is replaced by a new motivation: the desire to please God.

□ *Men.* Wrong attitudes toward masculinity cause many problems for men in our culture. One such problem involves *passivity.*

One morning years ago, I (Bob) overheard my name mentioned in casual conversation in the next room. A group of us from church were on a weekend trip to the mountains, and others prepared breakfast while I lazed in bed.

"Is Bob an aggressive driver?"

The question had been directed to a woman in my singles' group with whom I had been spending a lot of time. I held my breath to catch her reply.

"Aggressive driver? Bob?" I could hear her laugh. "He's not aggressive in *anything!*"

Her comment pierced me like a white-hot needle, her words almost too painful to contemplate. I felt like a complete failure, totally stripped of any shred of masculinity.

Was the problem really in me? Or in my friend's expectation of how a "masculine" guy should behave?

Perhaps some of both. Whether we like it or not, we are all impacted by our culture. We have been trained during our whole lives to expect certain behavioral traits from men and others from women. When these cultural expectations are not met, we experience rejection from others.

The solution is not to strive to measure up to the ideal man or woman of secular society. However, we can't go to the other extreme and ignore these cultural norms either. Some gay men almost seem to take pride in their ignorance of our culture's "masculine" pursuits, such as sports, cars and home repairs.

The balance lies somewhere in between. When I spend some time in the sports page, I feel more informed about what other men are talking about. I feel more confident in being around the "sports nuts" after church. When I sense their approval and enjoyment of being around me, I feel built up as a man. I feel more masculine.

When I take the initiative in a decision—despite the risk of ridicule or rejection—I feel better about myself. I like taking that role, and I feel more respected by others, both men and women.

Like myself, many ex-gay men have struggled with a passivity syndrome. We let others always take the lead; we avoid conflict or controversy at any cost. In the past I felt afraid of rejection, of making a choice that was less than ideal. I easily became paralyzed by insecurity.

Many gay men have a thousand hidden memories of past ridicule, of trying to take the initiative and being scoffed at. So it became safer to be passive and compliant.

Unfortunately, this compliance reinforces a homosexual identity.

What we esteem as the ideal (and lack in ourselves), we are attracted to in others. So an ex-gay male who is passive will commonly experience sexual attraction to outgoing, aggressive and confident men. Until that man comes to terms with his own passivity, such sexual attractions will continue.

Similarly, we must develop the parts of our personality that have remained undeveloped in the past. When we mature emotionally in our "masculine" and "feminine" character, we will take another important step in overcoming improper same-sex attractions.

Pursuing Godly Role Models

Once we come to the place of wanting to please God, of desiring to accept our masculine or feminine identity, we still may wonder, *Who should I pattern myself after?*

☐ *Patterns for men.* Jesus Christ is our foremost model of godly masculinity. He was a leader to some of the most roughly hewn characters of his culture. They would never have traded their livelihood for a weak, indecisive leader. Jesus boldly admonished the religious leaders of his day for their outward obedience and inner filth (Mt 23:25); he commanded rugged fishermen, "Come, follow me . . . and I will make you fishers of men," and they instantly obeyed (Mk 1:17-18); he rebuked demons, disease and storm-tossed waves with an authority that awed his disciples.

But Jesus also demonstrated other qualities not so highly sought after by men in our culture. He demonstrated his emotions of sorrow and pain; he grieved over the sins of religious leaders who sought only outward conformity to God's law (Mt 23:27-28); he wept over the pain of men and women he loved (Jn 11:35). He was affectionate and tender with children (Mt 19:13-15), and patient and loving with sinful people (Jn 8:11). Jesus is the supreme example for all Christian men who wonder, *What is the biblical pattern of masculinity?*

Besides emulating Jesus, ex-gay men can learn much from studying the lives of other godly men in the Bible. You might also want to visit a Christian bookstore and pick up a novel about a male Bible hero, such as Daniel or David.[5] Although these novels fill in parts of the man's story that are not detailed in Scripture, they can bring to life the biblical characters in new ways that you can relate to. You will see that these men struggled with many of the same relational and self-image problems that you do. Getting to know men in Scripture can be tremendously helpful in your character growth.

Other role models exist right in your church. In the past decade I (Bob) have been privileged to befriend several straight men in my church who have exhibited godly masculinity. They have been helpful examples, as I have observed their actions toward other men and women. As I have grown in my masculinity, I have earned their respect and love. This has been invaluable in bolstering my self-image as a male. We will take a closer look at forming these healing relationships with others in the next chapter on friendships.

☐ *Patterns for women.* Some women have pointed out, "Jesus is our role model too." This is true. Christ is the highest example of godliness for all believers, male and female alike. There is a sense in which males who model themselves after Jesus will become more fully masculine, while women who model after Christ will enjoy a deeper understanding of their womanhood. And in being transformed into the image of Christ, each of us becomes more godly, yet more human as well.

Still, as women, we need other women to help us realize the distinctiveness and full potential of our gender. As an eager new Christian, I (Lori) wanted to find the ultimate "godly woman" so I could model myself after her. I envisioned this paragon as a serene, willowy lady with her hair pulled back in a bun, working alongside her farmer husband, bravely trusting God's provision in the face of impending drought or locusts. (My prototype must have been Ma Ingalls from *Little House on the Prairie,* or perhaps Olivia, the mother on *The Waltons.*) While this was an image I genuinely admired—a strong but feminine woman—I needed a few more ideas of what the "godly woman" could be like.

I discovered that the Bible is full of women we can study, if not imitate. For example, Sarah, the wife of Abraham, is commended as a woman of faith and godliness (1 Pet 3:6).

This might lead us to envision Sarah as a pious, ever-righteous, quiet little woman. But the span of Genesis's account of Sarah shows us this was not always the case.

For instance, she laughed in disbelief when the Lord told her that she would bear a son. Then her impatience with God's timing prompted her to bully Abraham into sleeping with Hagar, an action she quickly lived to regret.

Sarah was a real human being, not an airbrushed, idealized icon of womanhood. Her overall life reveals a woman of courage and stamina, one who traveled with her husband from their homeland on a perilous journey in obedience to God. She trusted God even when her husband pawned her off as his sister and let her join Pharaoh's harem. She waited years to receive her promised son, growing in reverence for the Lord and faith in his provision. Sarah was a godly woman.

The more we study the women of the Bible, the more we realize that godly women don't just come in one flavor. There is Deborah, a courageous judge and leader of Israel; Esther, whose spirit, boldness and beauty saved the Jewish people from annihilation; and Mary (of Mary, Martha and Lazarus) who sat at Jesus' feet, soaking up his teachings.

Then there is Mary, the mother of Jesus. An angel of the Lord appeared to a teenage girl, informing her that the "power of the Most High will overshadow" her, and she will become the mother of the Son of God. Mary's response: "I am the Lord's servant. May it be to me as you have said" (Lk 1:35-38).

So many different kinds of godly women exist, yet each demonstrates this one uniting quality: a godly woman is *ready* and *willing* to fulfill God's purpose for her.

The beauty and excitement of this is that every one of us can be a godly woman. There is no single prototype, because we are not all called of God to do the same things, to be the same kind of women. Our femininity, as reflected in our unique personality, will be manifested in our lives as we eagerly seek the Lord, discover his will for us and set out to do it.

Friends As Role Models

Karen was hesitant at first to develop a friendship with Sherry, who was definitely heterosexual—a beautiful, confident Christian woman. She admired her so much. In fact, she would look at her and think, *That's what I could be like if I were healed.* Karen did pursue a friendship with Sherry, and she was open with her about her fears. Sherry was solid in her relationship with the Lord, and though Karen did become emotionally dependent on her, the two were able to talk things out and pray through any problems that developed. The dependency faded, and the relationship helped Karen become stronger and more secure in her own feminine identity. "Before I met Sherry, my standard uniform was a T-shirt and jeans, usually purchased from the men's department. Sherry never pressured me to change, but if she needed to shop for clothes, she would invite me along. I'd watch how she combined colors and accessories, and I'd think, *That looks nice.* Before long, I was trying on clothes and asking her opinion, 'What do you think of this?' Now I can walk into a store and say, 'This is me and this is definitely not me.' People compliment me on my appearance now; I've developed my own sense of style. Some of my friends actually ask me for advice on how to dress!"

TIME OUT

We have looked at the significance of accepting ourselves as male or female. This would be an appropriate time to release this area of your life to God in prayer.

"God, I thank you that my gender is not an accident. I know that you have a special plan for my life that can only be fulfilled through my feminine (or masculine) qualities and attributes.

"Thank you for creating me just as I am. Help me to become the woman (or man) you want me to be. Through obedience, I will embrace my true identity for your glory."

Most Christians—not just those coming from a homosexual or lesbian past—struggle at times with their sexual identity and roles as men and women. You will be able to share your struggles with others as you form meaningful friendships, which is the subject of our next chapter.

9

FORMING HEALTHY FRIENDSHIPS

*W*hen Todd walked into the counselor's office, it was hard to believe he had a serious problem. Tall, with thick blond hair and piercing blue eyes, his physical presence was imposing. As the director of an overseas branch of a major evangelical ministry, Todd projected an air of confidence and competence. Leadership seemed to emanate from him. Todd's life looked too good to be true. In fact, it wasn't good at all.

"I've been a basketball star, an 'A' student, and student body president," Todd told the counselor. "Many people want to be my friend. But no one—not one person—really knows me."

Todd had become a Christian during his freshman year in college, hoping God would remove the homosexual urges he had struggled with since age twelve. "That hasn't happened," he said. "But at least, as a Christian, I have an excuse for not sleeping with my girlfriends. Women think I'm so gallant. What a joke! I feel I would die if people discovered the truth about me. Yet I can't go on living in this loneliness."

Todd described recent trips to a large city near the ministry center where he worked: "I've started having anonymous sexual encounters. But I'm terrified of getting AIDS, and what if one of the guys I've had sex with shows up at the ministry center?

"My life is a facade, and it's cracking apart. I've always been the one everyone leans on and looks up to, the one who gets the job done. But I can't deny it anymore. I need help!"

*   *   *

Gripping the steering wheel with one hand, Mary Beth adjusted the volume on her cassette player with the other. Reducing her speed slightly, she peered out her car window at a two-story brick apartment complex. She knew what she was looking for: a small blue Toyota pickup. It should have been parked in the space for apartment #213, but it wasn't.

Mary Beth stepped on the gas, roaring her motor. Slamming her fist against the dashboard, she screamed, "I knew you were lying! I knew it. Elaine, you'll pay for this. You wait."

Mary Beth and Elaine had become best friends—and then lovers—almost immediately after being introduced by a mutual friend from the food co-op where Mary Beth worked. "The bond between us was instantaneous and electric," Mary Beth recalled. "And the problems between us came up almost as quickly."

As a teaching assistant at the local college, Elaine enjoyed a wide circle of friends in the academic community. Mary Beth enjoyed Elaine. Period. Though she pretended to tolerate her friend's other relationships, she kept a hawklike vigilance over Elaine's phone calls and, especially, her comings and goings. Their decision to share an apartment made it easier to do this. At first Elaine's ego was boosted by her partner's admiration and possessiveness, but she was starting to feel stifled.

Tonight, when Mary Beth called from work, Elaine had told her, "I'll be here all evening. I'm going to take a bath and go to bed early. Wake me up when you get home." Concocting an excuse to leave the co-op, Mary Beth took a quick drive to her neighborhood. Her suspicions were confirmed—Elaine had gone out. Torn between pain and rage, Mary Beth parked her car and rested her head against the steering wheel. "I could kill you for this, Elaine," she cried, unable to hold back her tears. "And if I didn't need you so much, I would."

Understanding the Patterns

Some of us understand Todd's approach to relationships: keep every-one at a distance, avoid intimacy, always be "in control"—and we won't get hurt. Some see ourselves in Mary Beth: craving an exclusive intimate relationship, and when we find one, taking desperate measures to keep it.

Still others combine both approaches: the more we want a close relationship, the harder it is to find one. Then when we meet someone who really does seem to care, we wonder, *Why is this special closeness so hard to maintain?* What starts out as a fulfilling, upbuilding friendship turns overnight into a bitter web of jealous, tearful accusations and ever-increasing demands. The "special friendship" blows up in our face, causing us to pull away, aching and devastated. *I will* never *let anyone get that close to me again,* we resolve, burying ourselves in work, activity and time alone. We pull into solitary independence, perhaps seeking comfort in masturbation, fantasy or anonymous sex but basically avoiding any real closeness.

This lonely isolation continues until once again, another "special person" appears on the scene who reaches out in kindness and interest. Like the dieter who has been starving for weeks, we fling aside all caution and plunge into yet another enmeshing dependency. And the cycle begins again.

In this chapter we are going to examine both sides of troubled relationships: defensive detachment and emotional dependency. Why do we get into these patterns, and how do we react in the midst of them? We will look at ways to break out of these frustrating cycles and move toward building healthy, Christ-centered friendships.

Defensive Detachment

Defensive detachment happens when we self-protectively close ourselves off from intimate relationships. Most of us who struggle with defensive detachment are the last to believe we have a problem. In fact, we tend to be the ones who are proud of not having problems. If something does trouble us, we feel sure we can handle it by ourselves.

Here are some attitudes and behaviors common in people who struggle with defensive detachment:

☐ *Anger:* door slamming, blowing up, the "silent treatment." We scare people away with our anger.

☐ *Humor:* sarcasm, put-downs, patronizing remarks, making light of our needs for relationship, minimizing the needs of others.

☐ *Isolation:* habitually choosing time alone over opportunities to be with others.

☐ *Self-sufficiency:* reluctance to accept gifts, food, compliments or acts of service.

I (Lori) think about times when I have stood in the checkout line at the grocery store, obviously pregnant, balancing a toddler on one hip and with my free hand maneuvering a cart groaning with groceries. "Would you like some help out with that?" the clerk asks. "No, thanks!" I chirp, as I wobble off to my car. Later, I always wonder, *Why didn't I just say, "Thank you, that would be nice"?*

☐ *Control:* being the one to ask the questions, not the one answering them. Avoiding group situations where we are not in charge (for example, only going to Bible study if we are the one leading it; only participating in singles' or college fellowship groups if we are part of the leadership).

☐ *Selective disclosure:* being open only about *past* struggles, ones that we have successfully resolved; being evasive or silent about current problems, even when people sincerely want to know how we are doing.

☐ *Compulsions and addictions:* workaholism, drinking, drugs, overeating, marathon TV/video-watching.

☐ *Weight problem and/or "dressing down":* ways to avoid attracting attention or inviting relationships (though certainly not all overweight people are trying to keep people at a distance).

☐ *Avoidance of touch or physical contact.*

☐ *Focus conversations on "topics":* to avoid personal issues or anything that reveals feelings.

☐ *Impossibly high standards for friendship:* no one qualifies or meets our expectations.

☐ For men: *a tendency toward temptations involving pornography and anonymous sex.*

☐ For women: *seeking comfort in isolation and fantasy.*

☐ *Emotional investment in pets.* Pets are wonderful; this is a problem only when they are used as a substitute for human fellowship.

Mutuality in Relationships

It is hard to feel intimate with people who will not allow us to give to them. It's as though they believe that in receiving from us, they are compromising their inner core of strength and integrity. Yet a healthy personality is one who graciously receives from others without feeling pressed to immediately "return the favor." Mutuality in relationships is important—giving and receiving in good balance, over a period of time. But when we feel we must rush to "even the score," we are missing the point of real friendship.

At a seminar on relationships, I (Lori) heard an interesting statement: "The outward sign of a hardened heart is not the inability to give love. It is the inability to receive it."

Sometimes defensive detachment shows up in people who seem loving and giving but who flinch or back away when people try to show love to them. People who have been deeply wounded are often surprisingly able to give care and nurturing. Their past even heightens their compassion for others. But the pain they have experienced was so devastating that they cannot risk opening themselves up to trusting or needing anyone. Vulnerability is too threatening; it might lead to more pain.

Underlying Hurts

What is at the bottom of defensive detachment? Hurt. All the "detached" attitudes and behaviors are walls of protection erected to separate us from potential hurtful agents. Yet behind these walls, we are numb and aching, often bitter. Life lacks warmth, color and joy.

As Christians, we can find peace and enjoyment in our relationship with God, but the enrichment we find in our "alone" times is meant to be shared with others. When we keep our treasures and spiritual insights all to ourselves, we stagnate, like a pond with no outlet.

Whether single or married, we are made for communion and community. In fact, we find our healing and our identity in Christ as first, we spend time alone in communion with God; and second, we enter into relationships with other believers. And, as we will see later in this chapter, a true understanding of solitude is part of the foundation for healthy, God-centered relationships.

Emotional Dependency

For people coming out of homosexuality, especially women, emotional dependency is a real hot potato. In fact, it is often a central struggle in the healing process and the one that is the toughest to deal with. Yet, confronting and sorting out the issues underlying dependency can bring freedom and wholeness in a way that nothing else can.

What is emotional dependency? Our working definition is *the condition resulting "when the ongoing presence and nurturing of another is believed to be necessary for personal security."*[1] In other words, when your worth, peace of mind, inner stability and happiness are anchored on *one* other person and on that person's response to you, you are emotionally dependent.

Lifeguard training includes stern warnings about how to rescue a swimmer in distress. Some struggling swimmers are so frantic that they lock their arms around a would-be rescuer and both die together. The expression "death-grip relationship" summarizes dependency pretty graphically.

Like defensive detachment, emotional dependency has some outward characteristics that indicate when a relationship is headed for this particular brand of trouble.

We are probably becoming emotionally dependent when we are

☐ *experiencing jealousy and possessiveness,* a desire for exclusiveness with one friend

☐ *preferring to spend time alone with our friend,* growing frustrated when we see him or her only in groups or with others present

☐ *feeling irrational anger or depression* when our friend withdraws even slightly

☐ *finding other relationships to be flat and boring* compared to this one

☐ *experiencing romantic or sexual feelings* leading to fantasy about this person

☐ *becoming preoccupied* with our friend's appearance, personality, problems and interests

☐ *refusing to make short- or long-term plans* that do not include this other person

☐ *becoming unable to see the other's faults* realistically

☐ *expressing physical affection beyond that appropriate* for a friendship

☐ *referring frequently to our friend in conversation;* feeling free to "speak for" the other

☐ *exhibiting an intimacy and familiarity* with this friend that causes others to feel embarrassed or uncomfortable in our presence.[2]

Manipulation

Since emotionally dependent relationships are a counterfeit to the true relationships God wants us to have, they cannot be maintained by godly means alone. To begin or maintain dependent attachments, we usually have to resort to manipulative tactics, which involve controlling another person or circumstances through deceptive or indirect means. Manipulation is the glue that holds dependent relationships together.

Here are some forms of manipulation that can be used to begin and maintain dependent relationships:

☐ *Wearing each other's clothing,* copying each other's styles

☐ *Using poetry, music or other romanticisms* to provoke an emotional response

☐ *Staring, giving meaningful or seductive looks,* or refusing to make eye contact as a means of punishment

☐ *Flattering,* especially by saying, "You are the only one who understands me," or, "I don't know what I would do without you"

☐ *Flirting and teasing,* using special nicknames, talking in a secret language only the two of you can understand

☐ *Offering too much physical affection:* hugging, touching, back and neck rubs, tickling, punching and wrestling

☐ *Combining finances and personal possessions;* moving in together

☐ *Giving cards and gifts regularly* to one person for no special reason

☐ *Making the other feel guilty* over unmet expectations: "If you *really* loved me, you would . . ." or "I was going to call you last night—but I know you're probably too busy to bother with me"

☐ *Keeping the other person's time occupied* so as not to allow for independent, separate activities

One cautionary note: Many of these things are not wrong or manipulative in themselves. Honest praise and encouragement, giving of special gifts, hugging and touching—these are enjoyable elements of a healthy friendship. Also remember that things like romantic gestures and a certain amount of exclusivity are perfectly appropriate in marriage, engagement or even a serious dating relationship, but out of place in a friendship.

Who Is Vulnerable to Emotional Dependency?

As you may have guessed—anyone. Given the right set of circumstances, pressures and opportunities, there is not a one of us who could not end up in a "death-grip" relationship.

Still, there are some definite patterns in how and when dependencies form. Usually two distinct personality types tend to gravitate together. One partner may appear to be strong, competent and wise. The other seems more unsure, more emotionally needy, less "together." In reality there are two needy people. The "stronger" one often has an enormous need to be needed and a huge appetite for praise and admiration from the "needy" one. Interestingly enough, the needy person usually controls the relationship.

To get a close view of a dependent relationship, let's look at Paula's relationship with Anne, which began one evening on a bus ride home from the Minneapolis bank where they both worked.

"About five years older than me, Anne was tall, blond, polished and confident—what I perceived as my opposite," Paula recalled. "Her husband had filed for divorce a few months earlier, and on our ride home she shared with me the pains of 'starting over.' Her candor encouraged me to open up about the devastation I'd been feeling since my mother's death earlier in the year. Both of us felt relief in being able to unburden and amazement at the instant rapport we seemed to have. We said goodby and made plans to have lunch later in the week."

From that point on, Paula and Anne were inseparable. They had lunch almost every day and met after work for coffee or hot chocolate before catching the bus home.

"I don't know what Anne saw in me," Paula said, "but her willingness to listen, encourage and help me seemed to have no limit. When I'd ask her what she was getting out of our friendship, she would laugh and say, 'You take my mind off my troubles.' I could tell she enjoyed her ability to talk me out of a bad mood or help me to see a difficult situation from a new perspective. She didn't even seem put off the day I confessed that I had fallen into a lesbian relationship with my best friend during college."

Anne and Paula spent much time at each other's homes. "Usually, we'd go to Anne's townhouse, as it was so much bigger than my cramped apartment. On weekends, we'd make a nice dinner together, then watch a video, maybe drink a glass or two of wine. One night we stayed up until 2:00 a.m. talking, and I poured out my hurt about my relationship with my dad, who had sexually abused me when I was a young teenager.

"Anne just held me and I cried and cried, comforted beyond words by her embrace. I never wanted her to let me go. That's when I realized I was in love with Anne. And I told her so.

"She looked at me with compassion and said, 'I love you, too, Paula. I hate to see you suffer. You've been hurt so much.' "

That night, Anne and Paula slept together in Anne's bed, cuddled next to each other, though their physical relationship went no further.

"I wanted it to go further," Paula confessed, "but I was afraid to initiate anything. Still, I felt this night marked a change in our relationship. *We're committed to each other now,* I thought."

On Monday morning, a dozen roses were delivered to Anne's desk at work, the card reading: "Thanks for being there when I needed you. All my love—Paula."

"I couldn't wait to see Anne's face at lunchtime," Paula said, "to see how she liked the roses." But at lunchtime, Anne was not to be found. Nor was she on the bus after work. That evening, Paula left message after frantic message on Anne's answering machine.

"I was terrorized," Paula recalls. "Anne was my lifeline. Now she'd disappeared. The pain was searing." At midnight, Paula drove to her house and pounded on the door. Anne answered, still dressed in her work clothes. Behind her on the couch sat a good-looking redheaded man.

"Paula, what are you doing here?" Anne demanded, clearly annoyed.

Paula lost all control and screamed, "What do you mean? Where were you all day—and who is that jerk in your living room?"

"That's Perry. We went out for dinner tonight. Not that it's any business of yours, Paula. Did you want something?"

"I'm sorry, Anne," Paula sobbed, "I don't know where to turn. I feel so lonely and afraid. I got scared when I didn't know where you were."

Anne softened. "Come in. Come in, Paula. Perry was just getting ready to say goodnight, weren't you Perry?"

Perry looked as if he were not at all ready to say goodnight, but he collected his coat, kissed Anne on the cheek and walked out the front door.

Paula stumbled in, visibly relieved and began telling her tale of woe. Anne poured them both a cup of tea and settled back to listen. It was going to be a long night.

Emotional Bondage

Every emotionally dependent relationship is different and yet, they are all the same. Almost invariably they start out feeling so good to both people involved. But as time progresses, one of the partners, like Paula, feels more and more "hooked" on the other's care and support. The "caring, giving" partner, like Anne, feels guilty and responsible for the needy one, yet enjoys the satisfaction of being the problem solver, the "hero" for the other. The compliments and flattery usually feel pretty great too.

Do you remember a toy called Chinese handcuffs, consisting of a woven, cylindrical tube of straw? You would stick one finger into one end of the tube, and another finger into the other end. Then you would pull, trying to get the fingers out. But as you pulled harder, the handcuffs got tighter. That's what dependencies are like: so easy to get into, so hard to break free from.

Dependency has many facets. For a deeper understanding of this subject, we recommend picking up a copy of the booklet *Emotional Dependency,* written by Lori and published by InterVarsity Press.

Is There Any Hope?

People who have been trapped in defensive detachment, emotional dependency or both of these wonder if they will ever be whole in this area of relationships. We encourage those of you who feel this way: don't give up. God has something better in store than a roller coaster of loneliness and guilt. Relationships with others are not something to be avoided and feared; nor are they to be an idol in our lives, pursued at the expense of personal peace and a right relationship with God.

As men and women from homosexual backgrounds seek healing for some of the wounds and traumas from their early lives, they find new freedom to make choices about relationships. Wherever we are in the healing process, we may feel the old "rules" of relationships are no longer applicable. But what are the new rules, if any?

Many women coming out of lesbianism want to know, "How do I have a normal friendship—especially with heterosexual women?" Men, too, can be just as baffled. "Straight men come from a different world than I do," said Richard. "Many of them aren't comfortable in relating to me at first. How do I break into these kinds of friendships?"

Before we venture into new ways of relating, we need to change our perspective on relationships, especially with other believers. Instead of seeing ourselves as isolated islands, we need to realize that because of Christ's work on the cross, *we are joined together already* with other believers on a deep level.

The bond already exists, as Ephesians 2:19 explains beautifully: "Consequently, you are no longer foreigners and aliens, but fellow citizens with God's people and members of God's household, built on the foundation of the apostles and prophets, with Jesus Christ himself as the chief cornerstone."

This realization gives me (Lori) a certain security, an added confidence in reaching out to other Christians. I no longer feel I have to "work something up" in a friendship; I only need to discover and develop the bond that already exists in Christ.

This perspective also gives me added confidence in working out conflicts with other Christians. Whatever crisis might develop between myself and another believer, we both have the resources of God and the Holy Spirit to help us toward eventual healing and resolution.

TIME OUT

One of the first steps on the road to healthy relating is to bring this whole struggle to the Lord in prayer:

"Lord, you know I've had problems with relationships. I've sought friendships many times for the wrong reasons, looking for things no friendship could ever give me.

"God, I don't want to go down this road anymore. I want to form friendships, not out of my wounded neediness, but out of my love for you and my relationship with you. Open my eyes to the relationships you want to give me. Help me recognize old patterns as they crop up, and help me move out in new ways of relating to others."

Solitude: An Oasis in the Desert

In learning to build solid friendships we need to cultivate our ability to find peace and nourishment when we are alone with the Lord and with ourselves.

Developing a capacity for solitude involves more than building a strong prayer life or regular time spent reading the Bible. It involves learning to relax and enjoy God's presence and to enjoy ourselves when we are alone with him. We learn to put aside striving and to take in the beauty of everyday life and the world around us. In solitude we cultivate sensitivity and a true appreciation for others.

In his book *Reaching Out,* Henri Nouwen captures the importance of solitude as a foundation for relationships: "Without solitude of heart, the intimacy of friendship, marriage and community life cannot be creative. Without solitude of heart, our relations with others easily become needy and greedy, sticky and clinging, dependent and sentimental, exploitative and parasitic, because without solitude of heart, we cannot experience the others as being different from ourselves, but only as people who can be used for the fulfillment of our own, often hidden needs."

He goes on to describe the strength of relationships built on inner security and solitude: "In this solitude, we can strengthen each other by mutual respect, by careful consideration of each other's individuality, by an obedient distance from each other's privacy, and a reverent understanding of the sacredness of the human heart."[3]

For the independent person solitude provides a place to breathe and regroup before coming back into involvement with others. For the person who struggles with emotional dependency, time alone offers an opportunity to experience healing and comfort from the Lord directly and to learn appreciation for one's own company. When time alone is welcomed, rather than feared, the anxious drives toward dependency lose much of their power.

Uncomfortable Friendships

The gay and lesbian lifestyles tend to encourage a self-centered approach to relationships. We look for a certain "type" of person, one who looks good to us, who makes us feel comfortable, who promises to satisfy our particular needs. But if we are serious about building healthy, Christ-centered friendships, we need to be open to relating to people other than choosing "our type." God knows what kinds of friendships we need to draw out our best qualities and soften our rough edges. Usually these are not the kinds of relationships we would design for ourselves.

Harry discovered this principle firsthand. Every time Harry turned around, he seemed to bump into Roger. At Bible study, choir practice, Sunday service—there was Roger. One Sunday after church, Roger asked Harry to have lunch with him.

"The only reason I said yes was because I couldn't think of an excuse fast enough," Harry recalls.

Roger was the last person Harry would have picked for a friend. Huge, slow-moving, slow-talking Roger, with the slightly bulbous nose and the crooked, shy smile. Roger was the manager of a local seed corn plant. Harry had recently left behind the gay scene in Chicago to take a teaching position in this small Wisconsin community. Though he had renewed his commitment to Christ and hoped to make new friends, Roger was not what he was expecting.

"That lunch after church opened my eyes, though," Harry said. "Roger had a gentle spirit and a genuine depth to his relationship with Christ."

The two men developed a solid friendship. Harry introduced Roger to C. S. Lewis, George MacDonald and other Christian authors. In turn Roger sparked Harry's interest in wilderness camping and backwater canoeing.

At one point Harry felt compelled to tell Roger about his gay background. Terrified, he spilled out his story. When he was finished, Roger looked at him with kindness in his eyes and said, "I figured that might be the case."

"Does my background bother you?" Harry asked.

"I admit I don't understand it," Roger replied. "But I don't have to understand everything about you in order to be your friend, do I?"

Harry thought for a moment. "No, I guess you don't."

"Too Comfortable" Friendships

What about those people we meet whom we instantly like—maybe too much? Should we run away out of fear that we will fall into emotional dependency or even a sexual relationship? Or should we take the other extreme, tossing up a quick prayer *(Keep your eye on me, God)* and then plunging full-speed ahead, caught up with the excitement of a new relationship? Unfortunately, there is no easy answer to this dilemma. If we are in a vulnerable place and the other person is not mature and stable, usually it is best to hold off pursuing this friendship for a while. But in most cases, the best advice is "proceed with caution."

What Does a Healthy Friendship Look Like, Anyway?

It's important for ex-gays and former lesbians to realize that no friendship is one hundred percent healthy all of the time. We're all sinners, and our relationships are affected by our sin nature, no matter what background we come from. But here are a few qualities that are indicative of good health in a friendship.

Healthy friendships are:

☐ *free and generous.* Though we may experience twinges of jealousy when one of our friends hits it off with another, basically we're comfortable in sharing our friends. We appreciate our friends and enjoy their company without the urge to possess or control.

☐ *built over time.* Even those friendships in which we immediately sense a "kindred spirit" need time to develop. The gay lifestyle can promote "crash and burn" relationships that start out at eighty miles per hour, feel great for a short period of time and then, at the first disillusionment, run themselves into the ground. A solid friendship is based on shared experiences and growing trust, and there is no safe way to rush this process.

☐ *not self-serving.* In healthy relationships, we desire to promote our friends' growth, encouraging them to realize their dreams, even if this means they are unable to spend as much time with us. Instead of worrying, "Will my friend still be available to meet my needs?" we trust that God will sustain us through any changes in our relationships.

☐ *directed outward, not inward.* Healthy friendships are not self-absorbed. Unless we're encountering a particular problem or conflict in a friendship, we rarely discuss or examine "the relationship." Much more time is spent focusing together on mutual interests or topics outside the friendship.

☐ *not mentally or emotionally preoccupying.* In a healthy friendship, we are not mentally or emotionally preoccupied with our friend. We do not fantasize about him or her. It's not that we don't think about our friends or care deeply for them—they just don't hold any magnetic power over our thought life or emotions.

☐ *built on strength rather than weakness.* In a healthy friendship, both friends call forth the best from each other. Though we have times with our friend where we can let down and be vulnerable, we don't try to *keep* each other in a weak, vulnerable place. We support our friends, stand with them in their trials, but we don't solve all their problems for them, and we don't expect them to solve ours. Healthy friendships are joyful, healing and upbuilding.

Challenges of Friendship

When we enter into any new relationship, with a man or woman, straight or ex-homosexual, we need a blend of faith and caution. Faith, knowing that God is undergirding and upholding our efforts, granting us wisdom and grace in our efforts to reach out. And caution, being aware that no other human being is completely "safe."

Women from lesbian backgrounds often are used to "all-or-nothing" relationships—total emotional and physical enmeshment or total withdrawal. "I didn't even know what a healthy friendship looked like," Nancy said. "I learned a lot by watching straight women in my church relate to one another. It amazed me how they were able to share deeply and openly with each other, expressing affection through hugs and touching, then walk away seemingly unaffected by the whole encounter.

"I needed time to get used to this blend of intimacy and casualness. Behavior that meant one thing in the lesbian lifestyle meant something completely different among women in my church fellowship. As my healing progressed, I learned how to interpret the 'cues' and sort out the differences."

Dennis shares his observations on learning to relate to heterosexual men: "When I first got involved in the church, straight men scared me. Their lifestyle couldn't have seemed more alien: what did I have in common with any of them? They were interested in sports, cars and women—hardly my areas of expertise.

"Gradually, I got to know different men in nonpressured settings—men's prayer group, weekly Bible studies, church-sponsored hikes or camp outs. I realized we did share something important: a common desire to know and serve God. My confidence grew as I realized that insights I had gained through my relationship with the Lord, other men found interesting and helpful. I discovered that most single men felt shy and awkward at times, too, especially in relating to women."

Dennis also found that, with heterosexual men, a small amount of intimate sharing could go a long way. "I didn't go out of my way to hide my background, but I'd let other men set the pace in how much I shared. As we'd get to know each other, questions about our backgrounds would come up naturally. I would answer questions honestly, but with discretion and reserve. It's the rare heterosexual man who is eager to hear all the gory details of an ex-gay past."

It _is_ possible to have intimate friendships with other men and women. It is not wrong to hope that our emotional needs will be met. The key is for us to _bring these emotional needs to God first,_ then _look for him to meet these needs through a variety of ways and a variety of people._

Many of our deepest needs will be met by God himself. We may find one friend who makes a great prayer partner, another with whom we can joke around and act crazy, another who needs our special brand of ministry and encouragement. Our lives are to be a mosaic of friendships and interests, not a puzzle made of two interlocking pieces.

Ultimately, God is the giver of all good gifts—including true friends. With his grace and healing at work in our lives, we can anticipate a lifetime of growing in the privileges and responsibilities of godly friendship.

10

MAKING PEACE WITH YOUR ABUSIVE PAST

*E*d was twenty-five years old when he began realizing the full extent of his past sexual abuse. He had always remembered the incident with his older sister when he was eleven. Their brief sexual involvement had seemed insignificant at the time.

Then other memories began surfacing one day when Ed was counseling with his pastor. He was talking about his deep feelings of anger toward his father. Suddenly he began trembling.

The scenes came in little pieces at first. His father . . . feelings of terror . . . memories of shaking every time his dad walked into the room. He recalled details of his father's violent temper and the physical beatings he received for the smallest infraction.

In the coming weeks Ed's memories of childhood abuse became clearer, and he began remembering sequences of activities. One of the most painful memories was the first time he had been sexually assaulted by his own father. One night Ed had been home alone with his dad. They were wrestling in Ed's room when his father pinned him down onto the bed. Then his father began groping in Ed's underpants, an act which brought a mixture of terror and pleasure. Ed enjoyed feeling his father's strong arms around him. But the other part seemed so strange and terrifying.

"I had a tremendous fear," Ed recalls. "Deep inside my heart, I knew what we were doing was wrong. But this was my father. He was supposed to love me."

After that event Ed felt increasingly isolated from his father. If his dad was not screaming at the rest of the family, he was isolated in his room, reading or watching television, says Ed. "He wouldn't communicate with us at all. If we wanted to see him, we'd have to go into his room and speak to him. This went on every evening that he was home, so I don't remember seeing a whole lot of my father."

The sexual activities between Ed and his father continued periodically for the next four years until Ed was eight. During this time the fighting between his parents was escalating, and finally his father moved out. Ed came home from school one afternoon to find his mother in tears. His father had moved to a neighboring state, leaving Ed's mother to raise four children by herself. Ed didn't see his father for the next ten years.

Then, in the sixth grade Ed began feeling a curious attraction to his gym teacher. "He was the most wonderful man I'd ever met," Ed says. "He talked to me like I was a human being. I felt like he really cared about me. And—this is something I realized much later—I automatically thought of him in a sexual way. Because of what happened with my dad, immediately I thought of sex. If somebody loved you, they had sex with you."

Ed started experimenting with his cousins and other boys after reaching puberty. At age fifteen he was accosted in the men's room at the local library. Soon he was going to nearby parks to meet older men. "It was just for sex, because I didn't think anybody would love me enough to have a relationship with me." His pattern of anonymous encounters continued for the next ten years until he sought help from his pastor.

Sexual Abuse and Homosexuality

Sexual abuse is common in the backgrounds of women and men struggling with homosexual attractions. "At least 85 percent of the women I counsel have been victims of some sort of abuse," says Darlene Bogle, an ex-lesbian and ministry leader in the San Francisco area.[1]

Many male homosexuals have also experienced abuse in their early years at the hand of peers, older boys or adult men. Several male leaders of ex-gay ministries estimate that fifty to sixty percent of the men coming to them have been abused sexually.

What is the connection between sexual abuse and same-sex attractions? Why does childhood abuse lead in some cases to homosexual involvement as an adult?

Effects of Sexual Abuse in Men

In the case of a boy abused by older men, sexual activity blurs the distinction between intimacy and sex. For example, a young boy naturally longs to be emotionally close to his father; when he is molested by his father or a "father" figure, these longings cause confusion. Is he wanting affection or sex? Are his feelings normal or perverse?

Some abused males have such an exaggerated fear of becoming homosexuals that, as teens or young adults, they commit same-sex acts just to prove they don't like it. But sexual stimulation in the arms of another man can generate new same-sex attractions, and these males get drawn even further into homosexuality.

Same-sex abuse causes confusion about the victim's sexual identity. He was the sexual partner of a man. What does that make him? A woman? A homosexual? Or less than human, "an irreparably damaged freak"?[2] The boy may grow up feeling vulnerable, weak and defenseless. He feels detached from his own masculinity—the exact dynamic that leads to a search for his male identity through sexual experiences with other boys or men. One researcher found that young males sexually abused by older males were about four times more likely to engage in homosexual activity as adults than nonvictimized males.[3]

Mark Sandford suffered the trauma of a violent molestation when he was five years old. The memory was suppressed for nearly twenty-five years. As Mark entered his teen years, he became aware of a physical attraction to other boys. He was small for his age and endured regular ridicule from other boys and also a physical education teacher who called him "Susie."

Ten years later, as a seminary student, Mark's continuing struggles with depression and homosexual feelings led him into counseling, where the childhood memories began to surface.

At the age of five Mark had gone to spend the afternoon at a farm belonging to some friends of his family. At the farm some teenage boys ran off beyond a fence into a grove of trees. Mark's parents had told him not to go out back, but he disobeyed. To his horror he found the teens in the grove of trees, circled around two boys who were engaged in homosexual activity.

Mark tried to hide, but the boys saw him and pursued him. When he was caught by the older boys, several of them held him down while four boys forced him to perform oral sex on them. They were so violent that he could taste blood in his throat.

This traumatic experience profoundly impacted Mark's life. He felt a crushing weight of guilt. He had disobeyed his parents in going out behind the house; therefore he must have been responsible for this horrible event. After that experience, he rejected his masculinity. Being male meant being like those boys who had tormented him.

Through counseling as an adult, Mark was able to resolve the inner turmoil caused by this incident. He was able to make choices to forgive, and the Lord empowered those choices and gave them reality. He communicated with his wife and parents about what had transpired in his life. Mark and his wife have continued to pray as lingering emotional effects arise from the incident. But, despite his past struggles, today Mark is a fulfilled heterosexual man, seminary graduate and ministry leader.[4]

Effects of Sexual Abuse in Women

When women are sexually abused, the trauma often leads to anger, rage and hatred directed at all men. These victims may develop a phobia of male-female sex which makes them vulnerable to the sexual advances of other women.

Connie is one example. She was devastated at the age of ten when her parents divorced. "I felt that my security blanket had been stripped away," she recalls. "Seeing my father leave us that day, I was so hurt." Connie stayed with her mother and two brothers at a relative's home while they tried to find a house to rent. During this time, she was sexually abused by her cousin. She did not know what to do, thinking that she might be somehow to blame for the experience.

About a year later her mother got remarried. Connie hoped that things would be better—but she was wrong. "When I was twelve, my stepfather started to sexually abuse me. I was so scared! What if it was my fault? How could I tell my mother?" From this time on, Connie didn't trust men. "If they didn't leave you, then they would hurt you."

Then Connie noticed a new element in her relationships. "I started having crushes on my girlfriends, although I never let them know. They never hurt me, so I trusted them and mistook that trust to mean love."

At the age of fifteen Connie had her first sexual encounter with another girl, Lynn. "We started out as best friends and one day our relationship changed to that of lovers. I knew it was wrong. I knew what the Bible had to say about it, but I rationalized our relationship, saying if it feels right, it must be right. My relationship with Lynn lasted for sixteen months."

During this time, Connie began drinking heavily to blunt the pain she felt inside. Her stepfather's abuse continued until she was seventeen. Connie was devastated when her relationship with Lynn broke up.

"I went a bit wild and started going out with different girls that I knew in school. I wanted to find love. I only found emptiness instead." Connie's rejection of men as a possible source of love and fulfillment left her with only one option: other women.[5]

Many women who have been victimized deliberately try to make themselves physically unappealing to avoid attention from men, which they fear will lead to further abuse. They feel very uncomfortable in outfits that show off their figures. They may begin to dress in masculine styles or in dark colors, wear little makeup, or avoid jewelry. Some gain a substantial amount of extra weight. Sexual appeal is a threat to their security; they minimize it as much as possible.

Common Misconceptions

Inappropriate sexualization can involve far more than just sexual abuse, however. Here is one counselor's definition of incest: "Incest is a betrayal of trust that takes a sexual form *of any kind*. It may be physical, verbal, emotional or all three, whether blatant or subtle, onetime or ongoing" (emphasis added).[6] Notice that only one part of that definition talks about a physical act. It is a myth that sexual abuse always involves someone laying hands on you. Abuse can involve the offender exposing himself to a child, masturbating in front of the child or showing pornography to the child. Other children have been forced to watch their parents engage in sexual intercourse or have grown up in a household where the parents thought nothing of being nude in front of their teens or adult children.

Sexual abuse can be *verbal.* An older neighbor tells you dirty jokes whenever you are alone with him. Or Uncle Harry makes sexually flirtatious comments when others are out of hearing range.

Both genders can suffer *emotional sexual abuse.* For men it might be at a family gathering. Suddenly you notice that Aunt Sally is staring at your crotch. You check your trousers, and your fly is up. She continues to look, then you begin getting sexually aroused. You wonder if there is something wrong with you. *What's the big deal? After all, she's only looking at me.*

For women the perpetrator at a family gathering may be your older cousin, who keeps staring at your breasts. You avoid him all day, but you feel his eyes boring through you at every opportunity. You feel violated, but you are not certain why the incident causes you such shame and embarrassment.

Resolving Self-Blame
One of the main aspects of getting free from past sexual abuse is resolving *self-blame,* the tendency to assume the abuse was your fault. Let's examine five damaging self-accusations and consider suggestions on how to resolve them, as explained by psychologist Dr. Melinda Reinicke:[7]

☐ *Somehow I caused the abuse.* This is almost a universal reaction among sexual victims. Why do we carry this feeling of blame? "The biggest reason," says Reinicke, "is that molesters want the child to feel responsible. They choose to see the child as seductive because that lessens their own guilt." It also keeps the child quiet about the abuse.

Ask yourself, "How old was I when the abuse began?" Then notice children that same age around you. Would you blame them if they were molested? Would it be their fault? It may also help to find pictures of yourself at the age you were abused to realize how little you really were.

"Yes," a victim may say, "but I went to my neighbor's house. I asked for it." No, it doesn't matter what actions you took; the older child or adult should never have taken advantage of you.

☐ *But I didn't stop it.* There is a reason for this: Molesters have powerful emotional control over their victims. In the vast majority of cases the offender is someone the child knows and loves: a parent or relative, someone in authority, a good friend or a neighbor of the family. Offenders have an uncanny ability to target children who are lonely, perhaps those who have moved to a new neighborhood, or children needing attention because their parents are experiencing marriage problems.

Also, in our culture children are taught to obey adults. A child does not like her hair washed, but Mom does it anyway. Johnny hates green beans, but Dad makes him eat them. We do what we are told as children.

Often victims berate themselves with thoughts that begin, *I should have . . .* For example, *I should have run outside.* But a little child can easily be caught and carried back inside a house. Or *I should have kicked and screamed.* But what happens in the typical family when a child has a temper tantrum? Children are punished when they exhibit such behavior. Don't berate yourself for what you didn't try. Instead, remember why you didn't try.

Some children use indirect strategies, such as going shopping with Mom whenever she leaves, so they won't be left home alone with an abusive father. Or they ask to sleep in their parents' bedroom whenever Uncle Terry visits. Children do the best they can; they don't have a mature capacity to reason out all the strategies that an adult might think of. So give yourself credit for what you did try—even if it was not successful.

If your molestation continued as you got older, you may struggle with the thought, *I was old enough to know better. Why didn't I protect myself?* The answer is "learned helplessness." Your strategies of prevention didn't work when you were younger, so you gave up trying. This is very common.

☐ *I feel guilty because sometimes I enjoyed it.* This is often the most difficult self-accusation for victims. It is important to remember that God created the body to respond sexually when it is touched in certain ways.

Upon being stimulated, a little boy's penis will become erect; a little girl will feel a throbbing in her genitals. This arousal is automatic—and does *not* mean the child wants the abuse. Once that powerful sexual drive is awakened, victims might pursue self-stimulation or activities with other children. They don't know any better; they are not ready emotionally for what is happening to them physically.

☐ *Why didn't I tell someone?* Children are afraid of being blamed for the situation. Or, even worse, they fear that no one will believe them. You might want to ask yourself, Who could I have told? And what would their reaction have been? Some children accurately decide that a parent can't help. Maybe your step-father molested you, but he beat up your mother all the time. How could she protect you if she couldn't even protect herself? Or perhaps your pastor abused you. Who would believe such a thing?

Often a child doesn't tell out of fear of the molester's reaction. Maybe he would be hurt or disappointed or even hate you. Maybe he said, "This is our secret. If you tell anyone, they might send me to jail. You wouldn't want that to happen, would you?"

Another reason that children don't tell is because they have never been told about molestation, about "good" and "bad" touching. There is not an openness with their parents to discuss sexual matters.

☐ *I'm not valued by God, since he didn't protect me.* It is normal to feel anger at God over your abuse. If you doubt this, look again at the Psalms. Many times David shook his fist at God, yet the Lord called him "a man after my own heart" (Acts 13:22). God understands our anger and loves us anyway.

Here are other destructive thoughts that are untrue: *God is punishing me for something* or *God allowed this to teach me something.* The truth is this: Bad things happen to innocent people. It's hard to reconcile that statement with a just and loving God; great theologians have been struggling with this dilemma for centuries.

God does not promise to protect us from all harm. Many Christians have died for their faith. But God does promise to be with us, no matter what we go through. And he hurts with us. "For he has not despised or disdained the suffering of the afflicted one; he has not hidden his face from him but has listened to his cry for help" (Ps 22:24). And, perhaps most miraculous of all, he is a God who redeems the evil done to us and robs Satan of any victory in it (Gen 50:20).

Breaking the Secrecy

Melinda Reinicke says that "breaking the secrecy" is a key step in the healing process. Join a support group for survivors of sexual abuse. You can find out information on local resources by anonymously calling churches and counseling centers in your area. Consider telling some family members about what happened to you. This is especially crucial if there are children currently at risk of being victimized by the same person, such as a relative or teacher. If your sister, for instance, has children that are close to the age you were when your father molested you, she may need to be aware of your past, to ensure that her children are not abused as well.

Some adult survivors decide to report their abuse to the authorities, especially if there are current children in danger. Some courts are awarding financial compensation to victims even twenty years after the abuse occurred. Of course, this is a major step that you should take only after consulting with a pastor or abuse counselor in order for you to fully understand the implications and risks of going public with your abuse.

The issue of thoroughly resolving your past sexual abuse is a big topic that cannot be adequately covered in this chapter. If you have been abused, we recommend that you pursue further reading and counseling on this important subject (see appendix B). Two books which ex-gay women and men have found especially helpful on this subject are Jan Frank's *A Door of Hope* (Here's Life, 1987) and Rich Buhler's *Pain and Pretending* (Thomas Nelson, 1988). Dealing with your abuse issues will be a key to finding true resolution of your homosexuality.

Verbal Abuse

As we mentioned earlier, sexual abuse can be verbal. But other types of verbal abuse, although nonsexual, can be profoundly damaging to our security as men or women.

In her book *Verbal Abuse,* Dr. Grace Ketterman talks about the destruction unleashed in young lives by such parental comments as "You'll never amount to anything," "Can't you do anything right?" and "I can't decide whether you're stupid or just lazy."[8] Years later, these messages still play in the minds of adults who can't forget the haunting words.

"My parents always told me that I was an accident," confessed thirty-year-old Sophia, a recovering lesbian. "Mom told me in high school that she had her tubes tied after my older sister was born. I came along three years later, much to my parents' surprise. 'You weren't supposed to be born,' they told me over and over. I don't remember how old I was when I first heard those words, but they have haunted my life for as long as I can remember."

Verbal abuse can also result from words that are not even spoken directly to the child. Dr. Ketterman tells the story of Billy, whose mother spent years yelling and screaming at her husband about his "bumbling idiot" ways. His father ignored the tumult, knowing that his wife's mother was also a screamer when her children were young. He simply hung on, hoping for better days ahead.

Billy's father didn't realize the damage being done to his son. As the years went on, Billy lost respect for his dad. And he vowed never to be like him. Billy loved his mother, despite her temper, and he wanted her approval and affection.

"Day after day," writes Ketterman, "this sensitive, bright and quiet lad grew more and more like Mom. He adopted her exacting habits of perfection, learned to share her skills and hobbies, walked and talked just like she did." When Billy reached puberty, he made a shocking discovery: He was sexually attracted to men—just like his mother. His masculinity had been damaged by both his mother's harsh words and his father's total passivity.[9]

If you were verbally abused as a child, it's essential that you come to terms with these old "messages" in your head.

☐ *Recognize the lies.* Are there recurring themes in your life, thoughts of failure, inadequacy and other negative self-perceptions? Write them down and ask God to show you where these ideas came from. Do you remember specific incidents that gave birth to these themes?

☐ *Reinforce the truth.* What does God say about you? He can tell you in three primary ways: through his Word, through his Spirit directly to your heart, and through other people.

The Bible is a special source of information on what God says about us, about his feelings for us, about his plans for us, about his desires and hopes and dreams for each of us as his children. As you read and meditate on its words, pray that God will help you apply and personalize its truths.

Sometimes the Holy Spirit will speak a certain truth to us in the midst of prayer or worship, or even during some "unspiritual" activity like jogging, walking, showering or driving. Pray that God will speak to you in his time and in his way.

Rosaline, a thirty-seven-year-old nurse, was deeply troubled about one aspect of her past abuse. She felt that if Jesus had really felt her hurt, surely he would have helped her.

One night Rosaline awoke at 3:00 a.m., troubled, knotted up inside and feeling worried. "God," she prayed, "I am trying to believe you love me. I want to believe . . . help me to believe in you." Suddenly the thought entered her head that Jesus was holding her hand. "I could feel the nail print in his hand," she said later. "In one moment, I *knew* he felt my hurt. In fact, he felt my pain so deeply that he took the pain upon himself."

Rosaline began crying at the joy of knowing and feeling God's love. "I felt so loved and so encouraged that I knew everything would be okay."[10]

Emotional Abuse

Another devastating form of nonphysical violation is emotional abuse. Although this can occur in both men and women, it is particularly seen in the lives of men struggling with homosexuality.

Clint's past gives an example of this "emotional-incest" syndrome. Clint's father was an alcoholic with a fiery temper. To make matters worse, he worked the graveyard shift at a nearby lumber mill, and he would frequently storm through the house during the day, yelling at Clint and his brother for making too much noise while he was trying to sleep.

Clint vividly remembers the time his father came home after midnight and couldn't find clean underwear. In a fit of rage he dragged everyone in the family out of bed. Clint, his mother and brother went to the basement and did loads of laundry for the rest of the night while his father went to sleep.

"I lived in fear of my dad," Clint says sadly. "I developed intense bitterness toward him because of the way I was terrorized while growing up."

Then came further rejection when Clint was a sophomore in high school. "Dad abandoned our family. One morning he drove off as if he were going to work, but he actually was running away from home. He left us with nothing. No car, no savings—just a stack of bills to be paid."

Clint's mother had just been hospitalized with an acute attack of multiple sclerosis; when she came home, she was bedridden much of the time. Clint and his brother had to work evenings and weekends to hold the family together.

Then Clint's brother joined the army and was sent overseas, leaving Clint to care for his mother like any "good" son would do. "I'd been programmed for this role all my life," he admits. "Mother had often told me that she owned me and that it was my duty in life to look after her until she was no longer living. After that, I would be free to live my own life."

After high school Clint continued to meet all his mother's needs: social, financial, emotional. "Everything but sexual," he says, "and I'm not sure if I've blocked that out. It might have happened, since she slept in my bed often until I was in high school, when my parents argued."

Clint's relationship with his mother had a major impact on his sexual identity. He felt thwarted as a man, locked in a "little-boy" syndrome by his mother's demands and manipulation. Clint's problems were magnified by his parents' divorce; he bitterly rejected his father as a role model. "I decided that if I did just the opposite of what he did, I'd probably turn out all right." By making this decision, Clint rejected his natural link with masculinity, which eventually propelled him into the arms and affections of other men.

Breaking Emotional Bondages

Moving out of overly intimate relationships within the family is a process which takes time and emotional maturity. Here are some insights which may help you:

☐ *Assess the effects of emotional abuse.* The first step to freedom is recognizing where "emotional incest" has occurred. The dynamics can be subtle. Sharing your family patterns with a counselor can help you sort through what has really happened. If you feel emotionally bound by a familial relationship, it is helpful to sort through how you ended up in this situation in the first place. For example, think about how this relationship has affected you. Write down the positive and negative results in your life. Finally, honestly answer this question: What am I willing to do to change this relationship?

☐ *Take small steps to disengage from the emotional entanglements.* This process of separation will probably require the support of another friend or counselor. Discussing any proposed actions beforehand with someone else will give you perspective; it can be extremely difficult to implement them alone.

For one thirty-two-year-old man this step meant moving from his parents' home into an apartment across town, which he shared with several male roommates from his church. For one woman it meant taking a job offer in another city. For others the first small step is making alternate plans (instead of automatically coming home) to celebrate Thanksgiving or Christmas.

Clint faced his fears in deciding to make the break. At age twenty-one he began wanting a life of his own. But when he talked to his mother about moving to a neighboring state to live with his cousin, she reacted with a predictable response of manipulation. In tears, she told Clint, "If you move, there's no reason for me to keep on living. I'll just stop taking my heart medication and following doctor's orders." She even accused him of deserting her "just like your father did." Clint had to see through the manipulation and take that first step of separating from his mother's life. Once his mother saw that he was serious, she stopped her idle threats and began making a healthy adjustment to becoming less dependent on her son.

☐ *Ask God for insights into the hurts of the other person.* Often, you will realize as an adult that your parents, for example, have many unhealed areas that resulted from their own hurts and even abuse as children.

Clint realized this about his father, who had been so angry and physically abusive. Talking with other family members, Clint discovered that his father had also been abandoned at an early age by Clint's grandfather. His father had grown up hurt and angry. He had done the best he could with his limited resources, including a lack of relationship with the Lord. The emotional wounds of Clint's father become manifest in all their ugliness when he had children of his own.

Seeing this aspect of his father's life did not negate Clint's pain, but it gave him insight into his father's actions, making it a little easier to forgive.

☐ *Recognize that maturity comes through making difficult decisions.*

Becoming disentangled will not always be comfortable. Recognize ahead of time that you will be called upon to make hard choices that will not be popular with the other person. This is the inevitable cost of becoming free from domination. It is helpful to keep in mind that God is always available to meet the other person's emotional needs. Pray that he will be close to that person and that he or she will come to desire his comfort and presence in a new way because of your increased absence.

Forgiveness

One of the most difficult aspects of making peace with an abusive past is the issue of *forgiveness*. Just the mention of the word can bring up deep feelings of panic and terror. Sometimes strong emotions result from wrong ideas about forgiveness, such as:

☐ If I forgive him, he can hurt me again.

☐ If I forgive, it means what happened was OK.

☐ If I forgive, I will have to spend time with . . . be close to . . . enjoy being with . . . act as if it never happened.[11]

Forgiveness is not a one-time act; it is a process that can take a long, long time. Be open to God's leading, but don't try to force this issue in your life, advises abuse counselor Cynthia Kubetin. "If you're not ready to forgive, God will help you to get there. If you can make a decision to forgive and if you can trust what God says even just a little, he will restore you."[12]

Forgiveness may need to occur on several levels, as deeper layers of hurt and pain come to the surface. Usually we don't realize all at once the depth of wounding and complexity of effects that abuse has brought into our life.

Renouncing Inner Vows

We must also take an active role in combating past abuse by renouncing inner vows and lies that we might have embraced in response to hurtful experiences. Here are some examples:

☐ I'll never trust a man/woman.

☐ I'll never be intimate with a man/woman.

☐ I will never give my heart to a man/woman.

☐ I don't need men/women.

☐ Men/women always _____ .[13]

Do any of these vows sound familiar? Ideally, they should be confessed to a trusted friend or counselor, then *verbally* renounced through prayer ("The tongue has the power of life and death," Prov 18:21). This prayer can be as simple or detailed as you wish. Here is a sample of a simple prayer of renunciation:

"Lord Jesus, I recognize that I have made an inner vow of [be specific]. I ask your forgiveness for choosing to embrace that lie, and I renounce its power in my life right now in Jesus' name. I choose to believe your truth about [be specific]. Help me to know and obey your truth. I ask this in Jesus' name, Amen."

The Challenge of the Past

Past events, even those as destructive as abuse, do not have to control us forever. Jesus died to set us free from our past. By his grace, we can become strong in the areas where we have been weak and vulnerable (2 Cor 12: 9, 10). Although the process of healing will take much time and effort, we *can* find inner release and freedom.

"I never thought I'd be free of the haunting memories of my abuse," said one woman. "And, in one sense, it's true. I can still recall the events, but now it's almost like they happened to someone else. I'm free from their power; they no longer control my life." With God's help, that kind of freedom can be yours as well.

11

DATING AND ROMANCE

*M*any years ago I (Bob) met a woman named Dianne in my church singles' group. She was young, pretty, single, dynamic—and interested in spending time with me. Soon we were going out every weekend to dinner, movies and Christian concerts.

As the months progressed, we spent much time alone. It was not unusual for us to sit in the car outside my house until midnight or later, talking for hours about everything going on in our lives.

I really enjoyed our times, but I had a definite idea about the dynamics of our relationship. *This is nothing more than a good friendship,* I told myself over the next year. I accompanied Dianne to her office party at Christmas; she came to mine. We spent an increasing amount of time in each other's homes, so she got to know my family and I met her parents.

Late one night Dianne and I talked until about three o'clock in the morning. We had one of those "spill-your-guts-and-tell-me-everything-about-your-past" conversations. I told Dianne about my years of struggle with homosexuality; she confessed to me a near-rape experience at the hands of a former boyfriend.

Obviously Dianne and I had a good friendship and we enjoyed one another's company. But there was an uneasiness in my spirit. Deep inside, I knew something was wrong. But I couldn't put my finger on it.

Several months later, Dianne confronted me. "I want to know where this relationship is going," she said and expressed the desire to see our relationship become more committed.

Outwardly I remained calm. But inside all my fears leaped to the surface. I realized that, even though I enjoyed Dianne's company, I had no desire to enter into a romantic relationship with her. We had been spending lots of time together, but I felt little emotional commitment to her. In fact, suddenly I felt trapped and I wanted out.

Within weeks we were no longer spending time with each other. Much to Dianne's surprise, I withdrew—suddenly and completely.

Looking back, my heart goes out to Dianne and all other women in her situation. Now I understand that our relationship was headed for problems long before I was aware of it. And I've seen many ex-gay men get into the same pattern of relationships with women.

Dysfunctional Dating

There are many excellent books available which discuss a Christian perspective on dating.[1] So we won't explore the general topic of dating; rather, we want to concentrate on specific issues and questions that are common to men and women coming from a homosexual past.

Let's take another look at my dating relationship with Dianne. What was the "something wrong" in our relationship that I couldn't identify at the time? I believe there were several dysfunctional patterns:

□ *Lots of exclusive time together.* Even though I never admitted it (even to myself), Dianne and I were in a dating relationship. I always labeled the relationship as "just friends," but the frequent time spent alone in each other's company is called dating in our culture, whether the parties admit it or not.

Other people recognize what is going on—even if the couple doesn't! Several years after I broke up with Dianne, I began spending exclusive time with another woman. (Yes, I repeated this same pattern several times over the next decade without learning my lesson.) Finally a mutual friend pulled me aside.

"Bob," he told me, "I'm worried about you and Judy. You're sure spending a lot of time together." He went on to explain that time invested in a relationship meant it would move in some direction: either toward a deeper commitment, or it would break apart (as the couple saw that a long-term relationship was not a possibility). Soon afterward, Judy and I went our separate ways—and I felt saddened and guilty for the unrealistic hopes that I had fostered in her heart.

☐ *Physical affection without commitment.* Another mistake I made in my relationship with Dianne was becoming involved in certain forms of affection (hand-holding and kissing) without recognizing that these activities implied a romantic interest.

Many ex-gay men exhibit a high level of physical affection toward female friends when they have no interest in anything more than a casual friendship. Their body language is speaking a different message than what they intend, which is misleading to the woman involved.

Here are some examples of behavior we consider inappropriate between couples when one person is not interested in a committed relationship: kissing on the lips, habitual back rubs, holding hands while strolling down the beach (especially if the sun is setting!), sitting close on a couch watching television with an arm around the shoulders of the other person.[2]

Straight men would not engage in these activities without experiencing romantic interest or even sexual arousal. But men in the midst of homosexual recovery usually have an underdeveloped sexual desire for women, so they enter into these types of behavior with little or no erotic feeling. These men are oblivious to their emotional effect on the women, then they are shocked when a woman begins to express a romantic interest.

Similarly, be careful about verbal communication, such as men praising a woman's appearance. Gifts, cards, flowers and notes are powerful expressions of interest. Use them with caution.

☐ *"Buddy" dynamic.* Another common dysfunction we have seen is the "buddy" relationship. This is especially common in ex-gay men. Many of these men have always felt threatened by straight men, but are very comfortable around women. As a result these men use women to meet the needs that they never found in male-male relationships.

In these unhealthy relationships there is a camaraderie that smacks of undue familiarity. The woman's femininity is sidelined, and she becomes "one of the guys." The quickest way a woman can disrupt these relationships is by expressing a romantic desire. This upsets the "safe" dynamic and the relationship quickly ends.

☐ *Parent-child dynamic.* Beware of the "mother-son" type of relationship, where the man is emotionally immature, wants to be taken care of and is totally passive. The woman in this situation becomes the enabler, playing the role of mother. She meets all the man's needs, becoming the leader and decision-maker. It's a unilateral relationship, rather than an equal partnership.

Another variation in the "mother-son" pattern is the ex-gay woman who acts out the "mother" role to maintain control. She is drawn to a passive man (whether ex-gay or straight) who allows her to dominate the relationship. There is not an equal balance of maturity, and this dynamic needs to be resolved before the relationship can proceed in a healthy direction.

☐ *Feeling out of control.* Another red flag occurs when you feel the relationship is controlling you—rather than you being in control of the relationship. When I was dating Dianne, I often felt like the relationship was pulling me along, rather than having a sense of any control. I "woke up" in the midst of the relationship, wondering how on earth I had gotten there. It was a similar feeling to waking up on a train, not knowing where the train was headed and feeling like I wanted to jump off.

Rather than feeling like the "caboose" of the train of your emotions, you should be at peace in your heart regarding a current relationship. Don't let it continue to drag on and on if it's going in an uncomfortable direction. Speak up!

TIME OUT

Have you spent time one-on-one with a member of the opposite sex on a consistent basis? How did you define the relationship at the time? How did the other person? How do you evaluate it now?

Other Principles of Opposite-Sex Relating

Many of you reading this book will be older than the usual age when men and women begin dating. It can be embarrassing to admit that you are thirty and have never dated. There may be feelings of fear and inadequacy. Where do you even begin?

Many Christians (not just those from a gay or lesbian past) find it too threatening to date someone whom they have just met. Therefore, a helpful first step in getting to know others is placing yourself in group settings where friendships with the opposite sex can occur without pressure. This can mean joining a home Bible study, music group, singles' group or volunteering for a nearby ministry (such as a counseling hotline, AIDS outreach, a homeless shelter or senior visitation program).

When you meet an individual to whom you are drawn in such a group setting, get to know that person first before moving toward dating. We don't recommend that you date to find out if he or she is a possible marriage partner; you should know this person is a possibility before even beginning to date.

For example, through becoming acquainted in a group setting, you can find out such particulars as:

☐ Is this person single?

☐ Has this person been previously married and divorced? If so, why did the divorce occur? Has the former spouse remarried?

☐ Does this person have any children?

☐ How spiritually mature is this person?

☐ What are this person's career and personal goals?

Some of the answers to such questions may immediately rule out him or her as a potential spouse.

Of course, disclosure goes in both directions. Through getting to know this other person, he or she is also able to find out similar facts about you.

Disclosure of Gay Background

We have asked many former gays and lesbians who are now married, "When should the person you're dating be told about your gay background?" Almost all of them have given the same answer: when it becomes apparent that your relationship is becoming more than a casual friendship. Remember, regular and exclusive time together moves a relationship beyond the "casual" friend stage.

Don't fall into the trap of waiting too long to share your past.

Relationships must be built on a foundation of mutual trust. If you find that you are continually delaying the inevitable announcement, then it's time to step back and reevaluate. If God is leading you into a serious relationship, your friendship will survive—and ultimately be strengthened by—appropriate disclosure of your past.

You may be willing to tell about your homosexual past but wonder how much detail you should tell. We recommend the following guidelines:

□ *Be willing to disclose the overall picture.* For example, men, don't say "I've had a few homosexual experiences" if you have had anonymous sex with dozens of men over a ten-year period. Be honest about the depth and extent of your involvement in the homosexual lifestyle. But don't go into specific details like names and places. Most counselors agree that this level of disclosure is unnecessary and also unwise.[3] The other person must also know if you have been infected with various sexually transmitted diseases, including the HIV virus. Women, be candid about recent lovers or current tendencies toward emotionally dependent relationships.

□ *Be honest about your current level of struggle.* Some men and women confess their gay background but make it sound like that issue was dealt with long ago and now they have absolutely no struggles or vulnerabilities. If this is not true (you are the rare exception if it is!), don't minimize your present level of temptations. As your relationship deepens, your friend can become a partner in standing with you against sexual temptation, someone to whom you are accountable for your actions.

One caution: It is important that you communicate clearly when discussing these issues. "Yesterday I was homosexually tempted" can mean ten different things to ten different people. Be specific about what you mean by "homosexual temptation" or "lesbian attraction."

□ *Consider the other person's family.* Another related question comes up frequently: Does my friend's family need to know about my background? That depends. How serious is your relationship? Are you casually dating? Or are you almost engaged?

Consider the family dynamics of your potential in-laws. Are they a close-knit family? Do they understand the power of God to change lives? Do they live close geographically? Have you shared about other deep issues in your life, other than your sexual past? The level of disclosure you reach in other personal issues (for example, your current income, details of a past marriage, disclosure of a past rape or sexual abuse) will help you determine when and if to talk about your homosexual background.

Another important consideration is whether you will want to be public about your testimony in the future. Are you interested in witnessing to homosexuals? Do you desire to disciple other Christians struggling with homosexual issues? Do you find it exciting to think that you may write your story someday for a magazine? Or give an interview to the local paper? Or join the volunteer staff of a nearby ex-gay ministry?

If you find yourself answering "yes" to any of these questions, then you need to face the reality of telling your in-laws about your past. Based on my own experience—and dozens of other people I (Bob) know—you will probably be surprised at the love and acceptance you find.

If you choose not to tell future in-laws, you will have to live with a constant fear of them finding out your "secret." Are you willing to have that wall standing between you and them? If you have really overcome homosexuality to the point of getting married, why is your past something shameful that should be hidden? Talking about what the Lord has done in changing your sexuality may be the most genuine glimpse of the power of God that many of your relatives ever see.

When Are You Ready to Date?

Some ex-gays are terrified of dating. Others can't wait to begin. What are some signs that a person is ready to consider dating?

☐ *Freedom from sexual immorality.* The person who is still falling into homosexual activities is not ready to begin moving into heterosexual romance. Neither is the person still enmeshed in a same-sex romance (even if there is no sexual activity involved). While there are no set rules, we recommend that dating be postponed until you have been out of the homosexual lifestyle for at least three years. If you have occasionally fallen into isolated homosexual encounters since leaving the lifestyle, a minimum period of two years of consistent abstinence is recommended before entering into a dating relationship. If you have struggled with inappropriate emotional dependencies, we recommend that a similar period of about two years' freedom from same-sex dependency be attained before you begin one-on-one dating.

☐ *General interest in the opposite sex.* Perhaps you are not interested in one particular man or woman. But you realize that you have an increasing desire to spend time socially with members of the opposite sex. You have developed some good same-sex relationships, but you find yourself looking for "something more." You're no longer content to only "hang out" with others of your own gender. This could be one more indicator that God is healing your sexual identity, making you secure in yourself, and now you are ready to begin encountering the opposite sex in social and dating settings.

☐ *You want to!* This may seem like an obvious question, but it's an important one to ask yourself: What is my motivation for dating? Too many people get pushed into opposite-sex relationships because of what others are telling them. You may be the last single member of your family. Other married relatives may be having children, and parents or friends drop persistent hints that it's time you thought about such matters. Other members of the church may be pushing you into relationships that you don't want.

☐ *Willingness to consider the serious implications.* You have weighed the facts about disclosure, and you are willing to consider the other person's needs in order to avoid dysfunctional dating patterns. Another factor is the willingness to recognize that dating may bring up new areas of your life that need further healing, such as mother-son or father-daughter issues and the ongoing effects of past abuse. This new context can bring further challenges, so be aware of this reality.

Entering into dating before you are ready can lead to the "sabotage syndrome." Some ex-gay men and former lesbians plunge into dating, then panic when things are going so well that the relationship is getting serious. Then they hastily withdraw, leaving the other person feeling hurt, confused and betrayed.

So if you don't feel ready to date, don't do it just to please someone else. Continue to pray for God's best in your life. If you feel called by God to remain single for a season of your life, then be confident in that call. But make sure the "call" is not arising out of your own insecurities of moving into opposite-sex relating.

What About Freedom from Homosexual Temptations?

Some ex-gays may imagine that they have to be totally free of *all* same-sex attractions before they can begin dating. We don't agree. Many former homosexuals have moved into successful dating relationships before every aspect of their past lifestyle has been resolved (for example, masturbation may still be an issue in your life).

It's really not much different from the heterosexual who has had multiple sexual partners in the past. He or she must deal with many of the same issues, including memories of the past and a certain vulnerability to sexual temptation. Many straight men and women have overcome immorality and then entered into a godly marriage without claiming to be free of every temptation from their past.

Quite frankly, if we waited until every temptation was gone, none of us would move into dating! At the same time it's important to have made significant progress in your walk away from homosexuality before initiating a serious romance. Perhaps you know other former homosexuals who are now married. Talk to them about where they were at when they began dating. Ask them if, looking back from their vantage point, they wished they had waited longer—or begun dating sooner.

By the time you finish reading this book, we hope you will have identified many of the key underlying issues that need resolution in your life before marriage is a serious possibility.

Wrong Motives

A former homosexual may pursue dating for some inappropriate reasons:

☐ *The rebound effect.* Trying to forget a long-term homosexual partner by plunging into an opposite-sex relationship. How unfair to the person you're dating!

☐ *The struggle to be straight.* Fitting into the expectations of our society by dating. Getting a date to squelch rumors at the office that you are gay. Entering into a committed relationship to get the local matchmakers off your back. These motives use the other person to cover your own social insecurities. They are not the basis for a healthy relationship.

☐ *Flight from same-sex relating.* Men, are you dating to avoid other men? Are you running to women because you are afraid of other men? Women, are you using a "comfortable" relationship with a male friend to avoid falling into emotional dependencies with other women?

☐ *Boosting a sagging self-esteem.* "Look at the gorgeous woman on my arm." Or for women, treating a man like a trophy of how attractive and desirable you are.

☐ *Using dating to feel more healed and normal.* Are you more interested in romance itself than the person you are dating?

☐ *Escape from negative emotions.* Some may plunge into dating to avoid loneliness, to get attention, to be distracted from emotional issues they need to deal with. Dating can be a temporary escape, but it is not a solution to unresolved issues in your life.

What If I'm HIV-Positive?

We believe that all ex-gays and former lesbians need to know their HIV status. Although former lesbians may have become infected through several means, including heterosexual intercourse, ex-gay men have been significantly more at risk of infection.[4]

The former homosexual who is now HIV-positive faces some unique questions and concerns. One of these questions involves opposite-sex dating and possible marriage. Does being HIV-positive mean a mandatory commitment to celibacy?

Because of the serious consequences of exposure to the HIV virus, anyone considering marriage to an individual who is HIV-positive needs to count the cost. In this instance the cost is extremely high. There is no known cure for AIDS, and evidence indicates that individuals testing positive for HIV eventually will develop AIDS symptoms, though the incubation period may be ten years or more.

Women considering marriage to a man with the HIV virus may find themselves in a vulnerable position. Once a deep love attachment is formed, objectivity about the future consequences of such a marriage becomes difficult. The woman may be tempted to underestimate the actual risk of contracting the virus. Unless one partner is voluntarily sterilized, there is also the risk of children being born to parents who eventually may become too ill to care for them. And such children are themselves at risk for the HIV virus.

One ex-gay man described his reasons for deciding against marriage, should he test positive for HIV: "My feeling is that marriage would be unfair to my partner under those circumstances. I might enjoy the benefits of her support and love, but she would very likely have to go through the pain of my eventual illness and death. And even with precautions, she might become infected. That's a risk I would not want to take. I believe an individual who is HIV-positive can lead a fulfilling celibate life, experiencing wonderful friendships and many opportunities to serve God as a single person. But I would not recommend marriage."

We also have discussed the issue of dating and marriage with numerous individuals who are HIV-positive, but who express a differing viewpoint. Some of them are involved in dating relationships. Others are married. All agreed that HIV-positive men and women should not automatically rule out marriage as a future possibility. But they warn of the extreme emotional pressures and possible financial hardships involved in entering such a relationship.

"There is no right or wrong answer in this matter," advises Carl, who came out of homosexuality in 1986 and found out he was HIV-positive in the summer of 1988. Soon afterward, he began attending a new church where he met Brenda. They started going to meetings together and their friendship deepened. Eventually, after seeking counsel from their pastor, they became convinced that God was leading them together, and they married in July of 1991.

"There is a deep commitment in our relationship," Carl says today, but he emphasizes the tremendous stress involved in being married and infected with the AIDS virus. For example, he and Brenda have decided not to have children, a decision that has caused them many hours of quiet grieving despite knowing it is the right decision for them.

Carl says that Brenda is an incredible source of emotional and spiritual support. "I don't know if I'd still be alive if I were still single."

Dean has also faced the "dating dilemma" as an HIV-infected man. He became infected through promiscuous gay sex while in the navy. He was diagnosed when his unit was subject to random AIDS testing before being sent overseas. Two months later he got out of the service and returned home.

Dean had grown up in the church but had gotten away from his Christian beliefs during his navy tour. After returning home he got involved in the college group at church and began meeting new friends. That's when he got to know Sheila.

"We developed a close friendship," Dean explains, "and I ended up telling her everything about my background and diagnosis. She was the only one who knew outside of my family."

At first, Dean and Sheila had "just a friendship," but after six months they started dating. "I was totally honest with her about everything," Dean says. After eighteen months Dean realized that there were unresolved issues in his life that prevented the relationship from going further. AIDS was one issue that was causing friction in the relationship. Eventually they stopped dating but remained friends.

Dean warns that some dating relationships can become a "romantic caretaker situation," which isn't realistic. The destructiveness of HIV disease and its possible side-effects (such as incontinence, chronic pneumonia, depression and dementia) require a solid, mature commitment, not a relationship based on fantasy.

All these men strongly emphasize the need to be honest about your HIV-status with the person you are dating. "The sooner you tell, the better," says Ross, an HIV-positive man who is now married. "If you've been dating four months and haven't said anything yet, you're already three months too late." If you say nothing and the other person finds out through someone else, he or she will wonder if you can be trusted with other important issues, he says.

The couple also needs to honestly discuss the possible health risks to the uninfected partner. One study of married couples in which one partner was infected with HIV found that 17 percent of the couples using a condom *every time* for protection still passed the virus to the uninfected partner within one and a half years.[5] There is a sober reality to be faced here—sexual intercourse involves risk, even when you are following the "safe sex" guidelines so frequently recommended for prevention of infection.

Ross and his wife have full intercourse, but they always use at least one condom (using two condoms gives added protection).[6] "Not using a condom is ludicrous," Ross says bluntly. "It's like jumping off a cliff and asking God to send his angels to save you."

Both partners need to understand that there will be increased emotional pressures related to the AIDS issue. "At times I struggle with envy toward those who are HIV-negative and ex-gay," Ross confesses. "I think, *Why me, Lord? How come those guys were more promiscuous than me but didn't get infected?*"

Ross and his wife have had to face emotionally loaded questions such as: How can we get future medical coverage? When should we tell the extended family about this health situation? How much life insurance should we carry? Should we consider the possibility of adopting children? Although he doesn't feel plagued with thoughts of death, Ross admits that there are days when he fights depression and wonders what will happen in the coming months.

We encourage you to talk with other couples who have gone before you into this relatively unexplored territory. Ex-gay ministries around the nation can put you in touch with other men and women who have worked through the same difficult decisions that you are contemplating (see appendix C).[7]

Other Dating Issues

Some dating issues that you face are unique to your background. But most of your struggles will be similar or identical to any other Christian. Get to know other singles who are dating and spend time with married couples in your church who can offer firsthand guidance.

Perhaps there is a couple who heads the local singles' group. Even if you don't feel comfortable with the college-age group (perhaps because you are older), seek out the leaders for some private counsel.

Get more than one person's opinion on your relationship. For example, if you are part of an ex-gay support group, one or two members of the group may react negatively to your desire to date. Are they discerning that you are not ready? Or is their negativity because they are personally threatened by the idea of dating?

"I remember when my best friend, Linda, began dating," says Sue, speaking about another former lesbian. "I had to battle feelings of jealousy. I was good friends with both Sue and her new boyfriend. To tell you the truth, it made me sad. I wondered how much time they would have to spend with me. I even dreaded the possibility that they would someday get married and move to another part of the country."

There are many excellent books on dating. Remember, most of the issues you will be working through are common to the human race—not just a manifestation of your homosexual background. So learn everything you can from books, films, friends and any other resources you have available.

12

GETTING READY FOR MARRIAGE

*T*he whole idea of marriage may be intriguing to you, but it just seems so impossible. You may feel totally inadequate to be a wife or husband. The thought of a lifelong commitment paralyzes you with fear. What if the relationship doesn't work out? What if you lose interest in marital sex—or never develop it in the first place? What if ... what if ... what if ... ?

Sound familiar?

If so, I (Bob) can relate to your feelings. For the first thirty years of my life, the whole idea of getting married filled me with a suffocating fear. Marriage seemed about as likely—and as difficult—as climbing Mount Everest. Whenever I got involved in a friendship with a woman that began moving toward romance, I ran in the opposite direction.

I was happy being single. My ministry work was fulfilling. My male friendships were great. Life was full of exciting opportunities. Why think about marriage?

Then something changed. As I hit my midthirties, I began feeling a sense of inner restlessness. In thinking about my life goals, I realized (to my surprise) that I didn't want to be single for the rest of my life. During the summer of 1984 for the first time in my life, I began telling others, "I want to be married . . . someday."

Is this also your dream?

As ex-gay ministries around the world have matured, increasing numbers of former homosexuals are pursuing dating and marriage. We know men and women formerly involved in homosexuality who left that lifestyle and have now been happily married for over twenty or thirty years. So what is preventing more ex-gays from entering into marriage?

Fear is the strongest reason why many ex-gay men and women don't marry. Many of their fears are common to all single people. There is the fear of failure, fear of parenting, fear of financial setbacks, fear of loss of independence and a whole bundle of feelings best summarized as "fear of the unknown."

Most of these common fears are dealt with in other premarriage books, so we won't spend time on them here.[1] Instead, we want to address the common fears among ex-gays entering marriage that are slightly different from the rest of the population.

Fear of Losing Control

For women coming out of the lesbian lifestyle, this fear is "The Big One." Especially for the woman who has been sexually or emotionally abused by men, marriage sounds like an invitation to her own funeral.

Heavy-handed Christian teaching on headship and submission in marriage only aggravates this fear. "Why would I want someone to take over my life and control me?" Mary asked. "I've always called the shots. It's been hard enough learning to be open and vulnerable with the Lord. For me, trusting an imperfect, typically human male is too much to ask."

Janine Puls, a former lesbian and support group leader, recalls several hurdles she faced before marrying her husband, Dan, in 1988: "I'd been really wounded by men through molestation and other abuse from an early age. As a young adult, the only comfort and security I'd found was in the arms of another woman. I hated men and vowed that I would never connect with one."

After Janine became a Christian, she studied the Bible and started receiving counseling. "I began to see God's design of male and female being complementary, reflecting God's image together. This was a whole new idea for me. My only concept of male and female together was a battleground."

Janine had to face her feelings which resulted from the past abuse. "I had to be healed just to want to relate with a man, to receive input from men. I slowly realized that because I'd been wounded by a handful of men, I had generalized all men to be monsters. And, in doing so, I had closed myself off to half of the human race."

With tears streaming down her face, Janine prayed, "Lord, you made male and female, and you said it is good. I don't understand this, but, Lord, you said it. Heal my heart to the point where I can be open to believe this."

Janine met Dan in college and felt he was someone she could trust. They became friends and began dating the following year. Then major issues began surfacing in Janine's life.

"When we began holding hands and kissing," she says, "all my horrible memories of past abuse and incest came to the surface. I confided to Dan about my past and he was wonderful. He listened to me and hugged me. His feelings for me didn't waver or change. This slow buildup of trust in our relationship helped counteract my fears of losing control."

Men certainly can relate to this fear too. If a man has had a protective, dominant, overly intimate mother, marriage can look pretty horrifying. He might fear being pressured into marriage by a strong fiancée who finds decision-making much easier than he does.

In marriage, both personalities need room to be themselves and to develop their potential as individual men and women. If one partner tends to be quiet and reserved while the other is more talkative and aggressive, this dynamic should be discussed openly.

Fear of Losing Identity

Starla Allen has counseled many women coming out of the lesbian lifestyle. She says that many of these women fear losing their sense of "self" in making a commitment to marriage: "When women think about marriage, they wonder, *What is going to happen to my 'self,' my own secure identity? If two become one, then I've lost myself.* They are afraid of being overtaken or swallowed up."

Take Marie, for example. Though Marie decided to take her husband's last name when they married, she experienced some trepidation. "Merging with William into a one-flesh union seemed like losing my identity. After our wedding I couldn't bring myself to register my name change at the Social Security office. In prayer I began to see how God used name changes in a positive way: changing Jacob's name to Israel, and Sarai's name to Sarah. I sensed that God was giving me a new name through my marriage. I wasn't losing something, I was gaining."

Fear of Sex

This is one of the most common fears among both ex-gay men and women, and it takes different forms. For many people, fear of sexual performance is the specific form of this anxiety; they fear that they won't be sexually aroused by their spouse. Or that their spouse won't find them sexually attractive. Or that they will eventually lose interest in sex. Or that lingering same-sex desires will leave them unfulfilled in marriage and frequently tempted to commit adultery.

In talking with married ex-gays, we have found that most of these fears are groundless. Nevertheless, some people's "sexual inferiority complex" is deeply ingrained. In many cases feelings of inferiority center around the size of a man's penis or a woman's breasts; others feel inferior in their body build as a whole.

These kinds of inferiority feelings can come from several sources. Taunts by peers, especially in the shower room at school during the teen years, can be excruciatingly painful and remembered for decades. Men who have viewed gay pornography may unconsciously compare their bodies (including genitals) with the "perfect" standard of statuesque models. Viewing pornography can reinforce feelings of physical and sexual inferiority.

In the gay lifestyle, especially for men, there is a continual emphasis on bodily appearance and sexual expertise. For both men and women, our secular culture is filled with unrealistic ideas about sex. Many of them are perpetuated by the media, including top-ranking movies and television shows.

Unfounded Feelings

Feelings of sexual inferiority common among many ex-gay men and women are totally unfounded for several reasons:

☐ *Body build and genital size have little to do with sexual satisfaction—for husband or wife.* For centuries, people of every possible body shape and size have found great joy and satisfaction in the act of marital love.

Typically men focus too much on their "performance" during intercourse as the index of their wife's sexual satisfaction. This focus is not necessarily valid. In 1985 Ann Landers published the surprising results of an informal survey. She asked her female readers a simple question: If they could have only one or the other, would women prefer tender cuddling with no sexual intercourse, or sexual intercourse with no affection? About ninety thousand women responded, and 72 percent said they would prefer to be held closely and treated tenderly with no sex. Of that 72 percent, 40 percent were under forty years of age.[2]

Here is how Dr. James Dobson, a widely respected authority on family and marriage relationships, explains the female perspective: "Women . . . less commonly become excited by observing a good-looking charmer, or by the photograph of a hairy model; rather their desire is usually focused on a *particular* individual whom they respect or admire. A woman is stimulated by the romantic aura which surrounds her man, and by his character and personality. She yields to the man who appeals to her emotionally as well as physically."[3]

Ex-gay men who are unduly preoccupied with their body or sexual performance do not understand what women find really attractive in a man.

☐ *A godly marriage is not built solely on sexual attraction.* A marriage is built upon the foundation of mutual trust, love and commitment. Both partners commit to love and cherish each other for life—no matter what. The vow says "as long as we both shall live," not "as long as we find each other sexually attractive."

Engaged couples may think that most marital problems are caused by sexual difficulties. "No, the opposite is more accurate," says Dr. Dobson. "Most sexual problems are caused by marital difficulties. Or stated another way, marital conflicts occurring *in bed* are usually caused by marital conflicts occurring *out of bed.*"[4] This is just as true for the former homosexual as anyone else. And, just to give a little perspective, consider this fact: After marriage you will typically spend the vast majority of your time thinking about nonsexual issues.

☐ *Lovemaking is a learned skill.* One ex-gay man who had been married six months expressed his views about sex in marriage something like this: "Becoming a skilled sexual partner is like learning to play the piano. You can't expect to make beautiful music the very first time."

Good sex is something you learn! It takes time, patience and practice, just like any other skill in your life. Don't put false expectations on yourself (and your future spouse) that you will somehow know exactly how to fulfill each other sexually from the first night of your marriage.

TIME OUT

Are you afraid of marriage? If so, which fears in the above section apply to your life? Do you want to overcome these fears? If so, what practical steps could be helpful as a starting point?

Prewedding Purity

Sadly, some ex-gay men and women compromise their moral standards before the wedding. They are so insecure about their ability to experience sexual arousal with their potential spouse that they allow affection to go beyond proper standards to see if they can become sexually aroused.

Some ex-gays have gone so far as to enter into sexual intercourse with the person they intend to marry in a misguided effort to see if they could "do it." Don't get caught in this trap. God's Word prohibits sex before marriage (1 Cor 6:18; Eph 5:3). The fact that you can function sexually once, twice or a dozen times before marriage proves *nothing* about your long-term sexual satisfaction in marriage. Some men and women have fallen back into homosexual activities after getting married and having regular sexual intercourse. So knowing that you can function sexually with your future spouse is not the key to a happy marriage.

There is a much better and more godly way to predict whether or not you will have long-term sexual problems in marriage, says counselor Paul Stevens. "Much simpler, nonsexual forms of affection over a long period of time are a better indication than having intercourse of whether a person freezes at the touch of the opposite sex or is genuinely responsive."[5] If you are free to experience appropriate affection before marriage with your beloved, more intimate forms of affection—including intercourse—will come naturally after marriage.

The Honeymoon

Everyone wants to have an exciting, romantic honeymoon. And, if you have browsed through your local bookstores lately, you will know there are no guidebooks available entitled *How to Have a Great Honeymoon—Ten Tips for Ex-Gays.* So here are some suggestions to help you get over the prewedding jitters about sex. (These pointers will especially apply to newlyweds who have never experienced heterosexual intercourse.)

☐ *Don't feel pressured to have sex on your wedding night.* This is a cultural expectation that can put undue "performance" pressure on a couple. Don't put that kind of stress on yourself.

Talk about the wedding night beforehand with your future spouse. What are your expectations? What does your fiancé(e) expect? You probably have not had the opportunity to quiz married couples about this very personal aspect of their marriage, but if you did, you might get a surprise: It is not like the movies, folks!

Even couples who do not bring added "sexual baggage" into their sexual relationship (such as homosexual struggles, or a history of incest or rape) don't necessarily have a satisfactory sexual experience on their wedding night.

When you have been married for a while, you will realize that the typical wedding day almost *guarantees* some problems that night. For one thing, if you have gone through a full-production wedding service and reception, you have just survived one of the most physically and emotionally exhausting days of your life. In other words, you are probably tired beyond words. It may be more appropriate to give each other a nice back rub, then go to sleep.

☐ *Don't travel a long distance on the first two days of your honeymoon.* Some couples schedule themselves so tightly that they have to arise at 4:30 a.m. the morning after their wedding day in order to catch a flight to some exotic overseas location. What a setup for potential disaster! This kind of schedule allows no time for an important and memorable aspect of your honeymoon—your first sexual experiences together.

Consider the possibility of staying in a local hotel for a day, then making that long plane flight. Of course, if you are planning a local honeymoon, you may want to do some traveling, but plan a light schedule that leaves you lots of time to be alone and romantic together.

☐ *Take a guidebook on sex on your honeymoon—and read it together.* There are excellent Christian books on the market that can be very helpful, especially for those who come into the marriage with no past sexual experiences.[6] Some Christians find these books too sexually explicit to read before marriage, but they make great honeymoon reading. (You get to try the things you're reading about!)

☐ *Pray about your sexual relationship.* God invented sex and he delights in your married sexual relationship. (If you doubt this, read the Song of Solomon in a modern translation of the Bible.) Commit every aspect of your marital life to him—including your sexual fulfillment. "My husband and I have found it very meaningful to pray together about our sexual relationship," says one former lesbian. "And, even in the midst of having sex, I often find myself praying for his emotional and physical fulfillment."

☐ *Be realistic in your sexual expectations.* "Almost every couple has to work out difficulties in their sexual relationship," say Kathleen and Thomas Hart, authors of *The First Two Years of Marriage.* "Developing a mutually satisfying sexual relationship takes time, a lot of communication, and considerable experimenting."[7] Here is another area where popular culture can lead us astray. Despite what you may see in today's movies, men and women do not necessarily know how to please their sexual partner without some experience and practice.

☐ *Communicate before, during and after your sexual experiences together.* Conversation about your sexual relationship helps defuse the atmosphere of a "performance," which will feed anxiety and reduce sexual desire. It is unrealistic that your partner will read your mind about what you enjoy. So talk about the manners and techniques that stimulate you and those that don't.

Marriage Myths for Ex-Gays

Some former homosexuals enter marriage with false expectations:

Myth 1: Marriage will automatically reduce (or eliminate) homosexual temptation. This expectation is based on the false idea that homosexual temptations are strictly a physical phenomenon, but having a sexual outlet does not mean you won't be tempted. For one thing, much of the dynamic of homosexuality is *emotionally* based. A wife can be emotionally vulnerable to another woman while her husband is standing in the same room, just as easily as when he is away for two weeks on a business trip. A husband can just as easily experience a same-sex temptation one hour after making love to his wife as he can five days later.

In men, homosexual temptations can be prompted by such emotions as anger, loneliness, frustration and boredom.[8] In the case of a woman, temptations toward lesbianism can result when something emotional is missing in her marriage, such as romance, intimacy or tenderness. If the pressures of being a spouse or parent push these emotional "buttons," homosexual temptations may actually *increase* in the married ex-gay who does not know how to resolve these issues.

Myth 2: Ex-gays and former lesbians make inferior spouses and parents in comparison to those who have never struggled with homosexuality. Nothing could be further from the truth. In fact, some former homosexuals are superior husbands and wives to the average person. Why is this?

Married ex-gays usually don't take their marriages for granted. They don't assume that problems will take care of themselves. They don't neglect their duties as parents and spouses. In other words, they work at their marriage and make its success a priority. One of the greatest marriage myths in our culture is the idea that "good marriages just happen" when a person picks the right partner. Wrong, wrong, wrong!

Doug Fields, author of *Creative Romance,* has talked with couples who are enjoying their marriage. "I usually find," he says, "that the common denominator behind their happiness is the principle of working hard at their marital relationships."[9]

Also, it's true that some ex-gay men lean toward qualities usually deemed "female" in our culture: they are often sensitive, caring, romantic, verbal. These qualities may not be highly esteemed by straight men in our society, but they are often attractive to women. A man with these qualities will get higher ratings in the marriage department than the man who lacks them.

Myth 3: Marriage will never be as exciting as gay or lesbian involvement. This myth may have some truth to it—on a strictly physical level. Specifically, it could be true if your sexual excitement was based on such factors as variety (sex was always more exciting with a new partner); danger (sex in a public restroom or park had the risk of arrest, thereby increasing the thrill); or chemical stimulants (alcohol to loosen inhibitions, drugs to heighten arousal). For the same reasons, a woman may not experience the incredible emotional intensity with her husband that she did in past relationships with other women. Also, many homosexuals supplement their sexual encounters with graphic pornography, various fetishes and other artificial stimulants that don't belong in Christian marriage: "let the marriage bed be undefiled" (Heb 13:4 NAS).

However, there is a problem with sexual "fireworks" that are artificially maintained: these experiences are governed by the law of diminishing returns. What was once a thrill becomes commonplace, then boring. Maintaining the same level of "sexual high" requires finding a more desirable partner, a new graphic form of pornography or a different form of chemical stimulation to capture that lost excitement of last year's sexual escapades.

In general, men are primarily excited by visual stimulation, say the experts. Women are stimulated primarily by touch. Ex-gay men may find that this common pattern is untrue for their marital relationship. Even if the ex-gay man continues to be vulnerable to sexual stimulation toward other men through sight, he may find that the principle turn-on in marriage is touch. That's why it can be hard for him to tell ahead of time how much enjoyment he will have in the marital bed, when he is prejudging his arousal level purely on sight (looking at his fiancée).

He may never have the same level of raw sensuality in looking at his fiancée/wife that he had with stimulation toward other men which was fueled by lust, not love. The lust has underpinnings of illicit sensuality and forbidden pleasures with which the marital relationship cannot compete.

There is a problem with trying to compare marital sex and illicit sex: the pleasure of sex is more than a physical thrill. There are emotional and spiritual components often forgotten in the gay scene. Married sex has added thrills no gay encounter can compete with. There are depths of emotions which increase through years of commitment, selfless love and emotional intimacy. And there is the spiritual element of God's blessing on the physical union of husband and wife.

Here are comments from men and women who have experienced both homosexual sex and the thrill of marital lovemaking:

Caroline: "My sexual life is much more fulfilling today. Back in the lifestyle, I was always trying to fill up an empty spot inside with my lover's attentions and our physical relationship."

Jim: "In the past I was always centered on my own needs. I took whatever pleasure I could get. Now it's different. I want to give pleasure to my wife. So sex is much more than just a physical release. Now it involves a whole new level of intimacy."

Joyce: "With my husband I feel secure. I know he won't leave me if we start having difficulties in our relationship. Sex is very enjoyable. It's so much better."

Myth 4: My spouse will never be able to meet my sexual or emotional needs like my lover did. Some ex-gay men and women struggle with this myth, because they have bought into the idea that "only a man can understand another man's sexual needs" and "only another woman can really know what I find emotionally and sexually satisfying." With commitment, communication and practice, your sexual relationship in marriage can be more—not less—satisfying than anything you experienced previously.

One married ex-lesbian made this comment: "A woman knows naturally how to please a woman better than any man would know. But a man can be taught."

What about our legitimate same-sex relational needs? It's true that we all have needs that cannot be met by our spouse. But we can develop healthy same-sex emotional intimacy in appropriate ways with friends.

One ex-gay man commented: "One of the things I really enjoyed after getting married was the new dynamic of relating with my wife as a couple to other couples. I'd known married people when I was single, but suddenly I experienced a greater depth of relationship with other married men. It was really exciting to get to know these men in a different way. It opened up a whole new world of same-sex relationships to me that continues to be exciting and very fulfilling."

As we saw in chapter nine, same-sex friendships are important, even in the lives of married men and women. A spouse is not supposed to meet every need that we have. Some needs can only be met by God;

others can only be met by our spouse. Other relational needs can only be met by members of our own sex. We put too much expectation on our marriage relationship when we think that our spouse can meet each and every need that we have. That's unrealistic!

Falling in Love?

One of the great romantic myths of our culture is that *men and women experience instant and intense sexual attraction to the person they will marry someday.* There is "chemistry" between you upon meeting. Fireworks explode when you hold hands or kiss. You will know, even after one date, "This is the one for me!"

Dr. James Dobson has an interesting comment about this idea. "Did you know that the idea of marriage based on romantic affection is a very recent development in human affairs? Prior to about 1200 A.D., weddings were arranged by the families of the bride and groom, and it never occurred to anyone that they were supposed to 'fall in love.' In fact, the concept of romantic love was actually popularized by William Shakespeare."

Real love, Dobson continues, is unselfish and giving and caring. "These are not attitudes one 'falls' into at first sight, as though we were tumbling into a ditch." Rather, they are something that we grow into and that process takes time.[10]

"Loving someone over the years is a very different matter from being in love. It is much less an emotional state, much more a choice," say Kathleen and Thomas Hart. "Falling in love is something that *happens* to a person; loving someone is something a person *chooses* to do or not do."[11]

Love Versus Sexual Attraction

Does this mean that we should marry someone to whom we feel no sexual attraction? Not at all. But neither should we go looking for a potential marriage partner who sends us into orbit with sexual desire before we even know their name.

In fact, ex-gays can enter into engagement with an advantage: They are less likely to base a relationship solely on sex appeal. When the sexual high of a relationship fades, a couple has to work through more mundane issues like finances, family planning, tastes in furniture and future career goals.

Love is not primarily a feeling; it is basically a commitment, says James Dobson. "This essential commitment of the will is sorely missing in so many modern marriages. I love you, they seem to say, as long as I feel attracted to you . . . or as long as someone else doesn't look better . . . or as long as it is to my advantage to continue the relationship. Sooner or later, this uncommitted love will certainly vaporize."[12]

Ex-gay men may not feel an overwhelming physical attraction to their future spouse, especially in the first months of their relationship. They should concentrate on building a solid friendship and an emotional closeness. Physical feelings will follow.

Ex-gay men who are happily married usually enjoy sex with their wives, but the majority do not experience sexual arousal solely by looking at their wife's body.[13] There are two other major sources of sexual arousal: touch and emotional feelings.

"I feel the strongest sexual desire for my wife when I feel most loving towards her," says Alan Medinger, a married man who has been out of homosexual activities since 1974. "Many times I feel those desires when we kiss, or when we are simply sitting on the sofa watching TV and my arm is around her."

Most ex-gay men do not struggle with sexual temptation for women in general, at least not the strong visual attraction experienced by most straight men. Indulging in opposite-sex lust may be called "normal" in our society, but it is not godly.

"An excess of visual sexual response is surely a reflection of man's sinful nature," says Alan, "and it is the cause of much suffering and dysfunction in the world today. Women are commonly valued much more for their looks than for their character or other attributes. Wives are too often compared, found lacking, and discarded."

So a lack of sole dependence on visual stimulation can actually be a blessing. Besides, as any married couple grows older together, there is less outward physical beauty to stimulate them sexually. "If visual stimulation is the only major factor in the [older] man's attraction towards his wife, they are both in trouble," Alan concludes.

When Two Ex-Gays Marry

We are familiar with an increasing number of married couples where both husband and wife are ex-gay. How are these marriage working out? Is this a healthy possibility?

It can be. We know one couple who were married for eighteen years before they both confessed to each other their homosexual backgrounds. Now this *isn't* the pattern of disclosure that we recommend! But we think that couples—no matter what their past—can be involved in healthy and exciting marriages if their past issues are resolved.

There are both possible strengths and weaknesses for marriages where both partners are ex-gay:

□ *Strengths.* There can be a greater understanding of each other's weaknesses. If same-sex attractions occur, both spouses will be able to offer support based on their experiences and past struggles. They will not be unduly threatened by confessions of homosexual or lesbian temptations, knowing that such feelings arise at times among most men and women overcoming a homosexual past. Both husband and wife will be less inclined to view their spouse as "worse off" in terms of his or her background. Although both of them may bring insecurities into the marriage, they can sympathetically support each other when those fears rise up in daily life.

□ *Weaknesses.* If both spouses are very unresolved in their issues, they could get into a mutually needy type of relationship, such as a "mother-son" dynamic, where the husband is totally passive and his wife makes all the decisions in the relationship. This "strong woman-weak man" relationship can reflect past hurts of both spouses, rather than reflecting a mature relationship of emotionally healthy partners. If an exchange in conventional marriage roles occurs, both husband and wife need to examine whether this is the pattern they really want, or whether they are avoiding more traditional activities out of fear and past hurts.

Marriage Fulfillment

Earlier in this chapter I (Bob) described how much fear I had with the whole idea of getting married. Then, in the fall of 1984, God showed me clearly that he wanted me to be married. I felt strongly led to begin dating Pam, a woman in my church with whom I had a friendship. Right from the beginning of our dating relationship, both of us sensed that we were headed for marriage.

I was overwhelmingly convinced of God's leading. We received encouragement and counseling through our pastors, and our friends were delighted. God confirmed our relationship through special verses in his Word. Looking back over our lives, my fiancée and I saw supernatural ways that God had worked to bring us together.

Then a strange thing happened.

All those doubts and fears about marriage that I had harbored in my heart for so long vanished like a mist in the morning sunshine. From the moment of my engagement until my wedding nine months later, I had a deep peace and contentment about the future. All my fears about marriage disappeared—never to return.

Now that I have been married since August 1985, I honestly wouldn't want to be single again. Marriage to Pam has been God's greatest gift for me, apart from his salvation.

Why is marriage so fulfilling? For many reasons, but here are three that immediately come to mind. First, I enjoy the companionship that my wife brings into my life every day. It's wonderful to have someone to share the ordinary events of my life, to build layer upon layer of memories which bind our lives together in a cord of shared experiences.

Second, I have more confidence in my masculine identity since being married. Of course, marriage is not a "badge of healing." But I see my marriage as a natural outcome of the growth that God has provided in my life. My wedding ring is a continual reminder of the changes I've experienced in the past fifteen years.

Third, as I experience Pam's love, I rejoice in the company of that "one special friend" that so many gay men and lesbian women are looking for—and have never found—through their homosexual relationships. My deep needs for emotional intimacy and companionship are filled by marriage. The struggles with loneliness, so common among single people, are no longer a part of my life.

Of course, I enjoy the sexual pleasures of marriage, and I'm thankful that the struggles associated with being celibate are past. It's very satisfying (and a lot of fun!) to express my sexuality as God intended, in the context of a lifelong commitment. There is purity, fulfillment— and no guilt. What a gift!

As a thirty-year-old man, I never dreamed that I would be married some day. Now I can't imagine being single again. I rejoice to see other ex-gay men and women whom God is leading into the same marital fulfillment that he has given to me.

13

GROWING IN MARITAL

INTIMACY

*F*rom the moment John met Lisa at college, he was attracted to her warm smile and outgoing personality. Soon the two were spending time together on a regular basis. It wasn't long before John asked if she would marry him. To his delight she agreed.

"I was so excited," John recalls. "Finally God was giving me a person to love, and now he was going to straighten out my life."

Unknown to Lisa, John had struggled with homosexual feelings since childhood. Sexual involvement with an older cousin when he was twelve added to John's confused sexual identity. He felt alone, worthless and unloved during his teen years. Fantasies accompanied by masturbation and nurtured by pornography gave temporary relief.

John's first homosexual experience came during college. He was devastated with guilt. "I hated myself and contemplated suicide."

After a stint in the army John returned to college to finish his degree. That's when he met Lisa and soon they were engaged. Finally John knew that he would be able to meet his sexual needs in a godly way. "I believed that this was God's will for my life and that it would solve my sexual identity crisis."

John's dream didn't last far into the marriage. "Our wedding night was a disaster," he admits. Lisa was a virgin, and John had never been sexually intimate with a woman. They were both "scared to death."

Their first sexual experience was painful for Lisa; another attempt the next day was the same. Afterward, John took a shower, sat on the floor of the tub and cried. "I had looked forward to this for so long and it was awful. The indictment of not being a real man because I couldn't satisfy my wife sexually tore through my soul."

Fortunately, their sexual experiences improved greatly within the next few weeks. But John's struggles were not solved so quickly. Before long he had returned to old habits of masturbation and visiting adult bookstores.

In 1975 their first child died six hours after birth. John interpreted the event as punishment from God for his past behavior and felt overwhelming depression

In the coming weeks John begged for God's help but still experienced powerful homosexual urges. He fasted and prayed, pleading with God to take away his lustful desires.

By 1978 John was the father of two children. But his family responsibilities did not keep him from indulging in anonymous homosexual encounters in public restrooms. He made promises to God about stopping his sinful behavior, then he would fall back into it.

John and Lisa were drifting apart. "We had a marriage in name only," he admits. "I had all but given up hope for my desperate desire for a satisfying sex life with her. The guilt and shame of my sin were overwhelming me. My cries to God for the past twenty years were answered with silence."

Finally, in quiet desperation, John made plans to commit suicide and find an escape from the misery that was tearing him apart.[1]

Wrong Motives

There are probably few people in deeper misery than those who have married with the hope that a loving spouse would deliver them, once and for all, from the struggles of homosexuality. Unfortunately, marriage is not the solution to gay or lesbian struggles.

However, whether or not you married for all the right reasons, God can redeem your marriage, says R. Paul Stevens, author of *Getting Ready for a Great Marriage*. "The Bible describes people getting married in all kinds of ways. Some couples were matched up by parents, others had a romantic relationship, some met through the initiative of trusted and godly friends, and in at least one instance a sinful sexual adventure ended in marriage. *Yet God took even poor marriages, or marriages for wrong reasons, and made them constructive*" (emphasis added).[2]

Awareness After Marriage

For some married people—especially women—homosexual feelings are not an issue until after the wedding vows. Then, for the first time, same-sex desires begin surfacing.

Madge was married with children before she met her new neighbor, Sue. Both were delighted to find that they shared a common faith. Because Sue's husband traveled extensively, Madge felt sorry for her and often invited her family over for dinner.

As time went on, Madge became aware of Sue's increasing dependence on her. Sue began reaching out in physical ways that Madge found awkward and frightening. They talked about it, but their relationship only intensified. "Sue became more dependent and increasingly affectionate. Any mention of controlling our friendship put her on the defensive."

Months passed. Madge couldn't seem to say no to Sue's increasing demands for time and affection. Eventually, she felt herself being increasingly drawn to Sue and began responding to her affectionate advances. Before long, they had fallen into a sexual relationship.[3]

A Failing Marriage

For most spouses, homosexual involvement is only one symptom of other problems within their marriage. Straying partners are usually lonely, lacking emotional intimacy with their spouse. They may face sexual problems which seem insurmountable, or feel frustrated because of superficial communication within the marriage.

All of these people feel a growing sense of desperation, of being trapped. One question surfaces above all the rest: Is there a way out of this situation?

Yes, there is. We know many married women and men who have struggled with homosexuality. Based on their insights, here are some questions to ask yourself as you walk through this difficult situation.

What Do I Really Want?

There are only three alternatives for the married man or woman struggling with homosexual desires:[4]

1. Walk the fence. This is the futile attempt to "have your cake and eat it too." Some might think it is the best of both worlds. A person can continue in the comforts and acceptance of family life but also seek sexual gratification and excitement outside the marriage.

Does it work? No, says Michael Babb, an ex-gay ministry leader in Wichita, Kansas, who speaks from his own experience. The first few years of Michael's marriage went well, then he turned thirty-five. "I saw my body getting older and began fantasizing about sex with younger men," says Michael. "I became strongly attracted to a business associate and we began spending several hours together almost every evening." The relationship turned into an emotional dependency, then became sexual. Soon Michael was ready to leave his wife, his job and his walk with God for this man. "I knew in my heart what I was doing was wrong," he admits, "but I had no strength to stop it."

Michael's guilt turned to depression. He felt "sick and frightened" deep inside. Suicidal thoughts plagued him. He lost thirty-five pounds and started drinking to ease the emotional turmoil. When his wife confronted him about rumors she had heard that he was being unfaithful, he denied everything.

Michael realized that the thing he had craved for years—a sexual relationship with another man—had let him down. *Finally, I'm in love with another man,* he thought to himself, *and I wish I were dead.*

Michael, and many others who have tried it, say the double-life syndrome is one of the most miserable, guilt-producing lifestyles that a person can pursue.

2. Abandon the marriage. A second option is to give up your marriage and pursue homosexuality. Find Mr. or Ms. Perfect and settle down in a permanent relationship. But, before you pursue this option, look around the homosexual community and see how many others have found this kind of commitment with a lifetime same-sex companion. The odds are overwhelmingly against you.

Rebecca Anne Johnston, women's ministry coordinator at Metanoia Ministries in Seattle, is a woman who chose this option. Married after her senior year in high school, Rebecca spent the next twelve years pretending everything was wonderful in a marriage she now describes as "abusive, codependent and dysfunctional." Then she found out that her husband had been unfaithful, and the façade came tumbling down.

Emotions that had been stifled down since childhood broke loose. Rebecca had grown up feeling inferior to her talented younger brother. When she was nine, her grandfather began sexually molesting her, and she put up emotional walls to protect herself.

Suddenly, all those years of stifled emotions broke loose. "I could not hold things together any longer. I was tired of the pain." Rebecca felt overwhelmed with anger, bitterness and rejection. "I felt worthless as a wife, a mother and as a person. My feminine identity was broken. I didn't know who I was."

Two weeks before leaving her husband and two children, Rebecca began a lesbian relationship with a coworker. "For the next three years, I lost myself in the gay lifestyle with this woman to fill the voids and bandage the pain in my life. I was addicted to her, emotionally, spiritually and physically."

In the fall of 1984 Rebecca reached the end of her rope. "I crashed to the bottom, worse than when I left my marriage. I wasn't eating or sleeping. My health was failing and I wanted to end my life. All the emotions I was feeling when I left my marriage were magnified many times over."

Out of desperation, Rebecca returned to her spiritual upbringing. She knew the truth of God's Word and cried out to him for help. Rebecca has been in the healing process ever since, although it hasn't been easy.

"There has been a great deal of pain, but more victory and healing than pain," she says. "If I am obedient to God, he will restore to me the years that the locusts have devoured" (Joel 2:25-26).[5]

3. Give yourself totally to your marriage. Initially, this may be the most painful and difficult option. You must give up your lesbian or gay pursuits if you have been active, die to your fantasies and dreams of same-sex love affairs, and break off emotional dependencies that compete with your marriage relationship.

This option may seem horrendous, terrifying and totally impossible. It may seem like a slow death, a denial of all that is meaningful and joyous to you. And yes, there is a certain death process involved. But finally you will be living in obedience to God's Word, putting to death the deeds of the flesh (see Rom 8:13), so that the power of the Holy

Spirit can reign in your heart again.

"The man who loves his life will lose it," Jesus said, "while the man who hates his life in this world will keep it for eternal life" (Jn 12:25). Jesus also gave this perspective: "If anyone would come after me, he must deny himself and take up his cross and follow me" (Mt 16:24). The call of the gospel is the same for all—whether or not they struggle with homosexuality.

So the option of abandoning homosexuality and embracing your marriage may seem like the most impossible choice. But go back and look at the other two options again. What God wants for you is clear. But what do you really want? Ultimately, only you can make the decision.

What's Missing in My Marriage?

Many of you are probably battling the temptation to commit adultery or form same-sex emotional dependencies. These temptations are a symptom of what may be missing in your marriage relationship.

For example, women are usually seeking to meet their emotional needs for friendship and security. "When a wife has an affair, she is generally not looking for sex," say Richard and Elizabeth Brzeczek, authors of *Addicted to Adultery,* "but for something emotional that's missing in her marriage: romance, intimacy, or perhaps tenderness."[6]

Some men are tempted by adultery for similar reasons. They are looking for an emotional bond and the sexual element develops as the friendship deepens.

For other men the motivation is purely sexual, especially for men who have a history of participating in anonymous sexual encounters. When they face emotional pressure, due to factors like tension, boredom, depression or loneliness, their old sexual habits return.[7] Anonymous sex is a temporary escape from the pressures of life.

TIME OUT

Ask yourself what is pulling you in the direction of adultery. Is the motivation purely sexual, an escape? Or are there underlying emotional needs you feel are not being met by your spouse? As you begin to identify these needs, you will take the first step out of the isolation and frustration plaguing your marriage.

Unmet emotional needs cannot just be ignored. It is essential that you take concrete steps to meet those needs in proper, godly ways. All of us have same-sex needs which cannot be met by our spouse. I (Bob) am part of a four-man accountability group which meets monthly. Over the months, each of us has been able to become increasingly vulnerable about our struggles and concerns as married Christian men.

I know other ex-gay men who are able to share their lives in the context of a Bible study or monthly prayer meeting connected with their church. Other married women and men have joined a support group sponsored by an ex-gay ministry (see appendix C).

Some take the risk (and it *is* a risk!) of sharing their lesbian or gay struggles with one or two other same-sex friends in the church. There is need for caution here. We recommend that *more than one person* should provide emotional support and accountability. There is a great danger of "burning out" one person, of forming a codependent relationship, of becoming overly emotionally entangled with a support system of just one person.

What Am I Willing to Change in Myself?

In any difficult marriage situation, factors in both husband and wife may be contributing to the problems. However, for the sake of healing your marriage, it serves no purpose to focus solely on what is wrong with your partner. Even if your spouse's actions, words, feelings or decisions are hindering your marriage, realize that—for now—change must center on you, not your partner.

It's easy to focus on "the problem," to blame homosexuality for all marital problems. But, in the years that we have observed marriages in trouble where one partner is ex-gay, we've made an interesting discovery: many marital struggles have little to do with homosexuality. Rather, they touch on deeper issues such as laziness, selfishness, emotional immaturity, financial irresponsibility, lack of commitment and other common problems in *any* rocky marriage. Pray that God will begin exposing and healing these types of issues in your life.

Have I Been Honest with My Spouse?

Some married men and women dealing with homosexuality have never told another person about their struggles. On this subject, the vast majority of Christian counselors agree: *To regain a healthy marriage, you must tell your spouse about your gay or lesbian struggles.* Of course, the thought of informing your husband or wife can be terrifying, and you may fear that the revelation will destroy your marriage.

But here are some reasons why we believe sharing this problem with your spouse is so important:

☐ *Emotional intimacy—an important element in a successful marriage—is based on honesty.* How can your marriage thrive when you are withholding such an important part of yourself from your mate? The highest gift in marriage, says one couple, is the "gift of the *self,* which can only be given if one is willing to open one's heart to the other."[8]

To gain another perspective, turn the question around. Wouldn't you want to know if your mate was struggling with a major problem that threatened to destroy your marriage?

☐ *Accountability is one of the keys to overcoming sin.* "Confess your sins to each other and pray for each other so that you may be healed" (Jas 5:16). If your partner has access to this area of your life, you will find a new strength to resist temptation. If your spouse is a Christian, he or she can become your most important prayer supporter in this area too.

Your spouse must know if you have been sexually unfaithful since marriage. This is especially crucial if you are currently struggling with a sexual or emotionally dependent relationship outside the marriage. It is unrealistic and naive to think that you can repair your marriage without your spouse ever finding out about your past or current activities.

☐ *Confession is an important step in the process of repentance.* "If we confess our sins," the Bible says, "he [God] is faithful and just and will forgive us our sins and purify us from all unrighteousness" (1 Jn 1:9). But can't we just confess our sins to God alone? Not in this case, because we have sinned *against our spouse* in harboring illicit desires and pursuing ungodly relationships outside the marriage covenant. If we have broken our marriage vows, we must bring that transgression "into the light" to experience forgiveness from our spouse.

Doug, a former pastor who lost his church because of two ongoing heterosexual affairs, began to sense his life being restored when he confessed the whole sordid mess to his wife, Sally.

"I opened my life to everything I had done," Doug said. "I laid it all out. The lies, the deception. Though she cried, she handled it extremely well. She never demanded details, though I was prepared to give her every detail, anything she asked. It was a great catharsis, though very painful for Sally and especially painful for me.

"For the first time in my life, however, I realized that if our lives and marriage could be saved, it would have to be through honesty."

Doug made a lifetime pledge. "There was an act of my will that I would never again let anything come into our relationship that I could not share with her. Anything."

Doug and Sally saved their marriage by making this commitment to walk in the truth with each other. "Adultery alone does not necessarily destroy the marriage," Doug said. "We were able to handle the adultery when we brought it into the light. Every man has flaws and sins. It is only when you keep it in the darkness that sin grows and multiplies. If it is brought into the light, then there is help for it."[9]

☐ *Confession enables both partners in the marriage to find help in dealing with their respective issues.* In many cases the spouse is already aware that something is wrong in the marriage and may be very unhappy—but doesn't know what to do about the situation. Sometimes women have been drawn to men who turn out to be gay, then they find themselves in a marriage that is empty of romantic love.

John, whose story began this chapter, started to climb out of his black pit of despair when he landed in the hospital with an apparent heart attack. For the first time in his life, he admitted that he needed help and that he was helpless in his own strength. He cried out to God for help.

Then, for the first time, he was honest with his wife about his homosexual struggles.

"One Sunday afternoon, I lay on the bed next to Lisa, whom I loved more than anyone, and struggled to put into words the past thirty-eight years of hurt, pain and confusion. We wept for days following that confession."

John and Lisa began marriage counseling together, and John began attending a support group for men struggling with homosexuality. Although he still has deep issues to work through, John is finally seeing some light at the end of his dark tunnel.

"I have found strength to share my struggle with my family, many friends and most importantly, my children," he says. "I have felt God's love expressed through others in so many loving ways." John's climb out of hopelessness began when he shared his struggles with others.

Madge and Sue began finding some answers to their dilemma when Madge confessed their lesbian relationship to a Christian friend. Although it took months of effort amid many tears, they were able to redeem their relationship with much help from their friend.

□ *Honesty is necessary because of potential serious health risks to your spouse.* Numerous sexually transmitted diseases can be caught through even one act of infidelity. The most serious, of course, is AIDS. If you have been sexually active outside your marriage even once in the past ten years, you *must* be tested for HIV before resuming sexual relations with your spouse. This is a matter of life and death.[10]

There is no such thing as totally "safe sex." Even with use of condoms, there is a certain risk of infection if one partner has the HIV virus.[11] Anonymous testing is available in most larger towns and cities. A physician or staff members at a local health clinic can answer your questions about HIV and other sexual infections.[12]

If you are infected with AIDS, this does not mean the automatic end of your marriage. But your spouse must know your health situation, and you must both be aware of the risks involved if you decide to continue your sexual relationship. This situation—a Christian marriage where one partner is infected with HIV—may have been rare a few years ago, but it is growing more common all the time.

Practicing Preventative Maintenance

□ *Focus on your partner's emotional needs.* In his book *His Needs, Her Needs,* Willard Harley describes the one principle that can restore a fractured marriage: "Become aware of each other's needs and learn to meet them."[13] Each of us can benefit from setting aside time with our spouse to honestly identify and share our deepest emotional needs. One man told his wife, "I need to sense your confidence in me, even when I'm wavering in an area such as decision-making." A former lesbian explained to her husband, "I need you not to pressure me when I'm working through some deep emotional issue. When I know you're there, supporting me, letting me take my time, I'm able to resolve things much more quickly. And I feel loved by you in the process."

☐ *Thank God for your marriage.* Even though you have had problems with homosexuality, you have undoubtedly experienced many of the joys and blessings of married life: establishing a home together, heterosexual sex, perhaps children. Ask God to bring back to your mind and heart the joys, the good experiences from earlier in your marriage.[14]

☐ *Learn your limits in same-sex relationships.* Most of us are aware of our areas of weakness to sexual temptation. For men it may be a certain look or type of man who triggers our temptation cycle. For women we may be consistently drawn to a certain type of woman who is older, motherly, deeply nurturing.

"If a certain person arouses feelings in you that are ungodly," advises Lois Mowday, author of *The Snare,* "don't feed those thoughts by manipulating ways to be around that individual. If it is someone you cannot help being around, such as a coworker, don't feed your weakness by becoming intimate friends."[15] And don't rationalize an inappropriate relationship that is becoming sexualized or overly close emotionally.

☐ *Remain committed in your mind and will.* Your marriage is based on a commitment made before God, not your feelings. Love based solely on feelings is unstable and a poor foundation for marriage. Pray that God will enable you to make this decision to love. Jesus is the source of love and the example of perfect love. Seek him diligently for the strength and ability to put your spouse first.

14

A VISION FOR THE FUTURE

*T*he change process is comparable to climbing the stairs when the end is not clearly visible," says Dutch psychologist Gerard van den Aardweg in his book *Homosexuality and Hope*. "You do not exactly know where you will end up; but every stair climbed means improvement, progress."[1]

Yes, for the rest of our lives we will be "climbing stairs" and facing new challenges. Many of our problems, however, will have nothing to do with homosexual issues. But some of them may be a reminder of our past struggles in the area of our sexuality.

Moving Beyond Labels
Those of us who have been around ex-gay ministry for years have noticed an interesting phenomenon. After men and women have been around a ministry for a period of several years, many of them begin developing a distaste for the label "ex-gay" or "ex-lesbian." They find that these labels no longer describe their lives, their relationships or their visions for the future. Such terms as *former homosexual* or *former lesbian* are based on who they used to be, not who they are now.

These labels begin to feel restrictive, instead of liberating. Just as a snake must shed its old skin in order to keep growing, so the people shedding old self-imposed labels of "ex-gay" or "ex-lesbian" are showing signs of significant forward progress.[2]

"I have trouble with the term 'ex-lesbian,' " says one woman, now married with two children. "I simply cannot describe the Lord's work in me primarily in a statement of what I'm *not.* It's too negative. No matter how much people talk about their deliverance, until they feel the truth of being a 'new creation' [2 Cor 5:17], I'm afraid there will be a tendency to hold onto the past."

Those who insist on hanging onto the old identity may actually be resisting what God is trying to do in their lives. Some men and women formerly involved in gay or lesbian activities become stuck on a level of growth that some have dubbed "the ex-gay plateau."

Andy Comiskey, director of Desert Stream Ministries in Los Angeles, has this to say about the plateau: "Ex-gay ministries run the risk of creating a distinct subculture. Composed solely of individuals seeking to come out of homosexuality, this subculture replaced the gay lifestyle as an alternative community."[3]

Forming both same-sex and opposite-sex friendships with individuals who do not share our homosexual background is extremely important in attaining a healthy environment for emotional and spiritual growth. Those men and women who surround themselves only with ex-gay friends find that there is a subtle tendency to keep thinking in a "we-they" mentality. "We" are those of us with a homosexual background; "they" are Christians who have always been straight. And we restrict our relationships to other former homosexuals who "really understand" our issues and struggles.

There is a danger in this exclusive mentality. "When we cut ourselves off from the church at large," says Andy, "we minimize the reality that Christ—not our sexual background—is the basis for our identification with the believing community."[4]

This type of exclusivity hinders our relational growth too. Reaching beyond the ex-gay crowd for supportive friendships is like playing tennis with someone who has a better backhand. The game is no longer safe and easy; we are forced to stretch our skills to keep up, and we end up being a stronger and more mature tennis player as a result. But we have something to offer too—perhaps a better lob shot.

So the other player also benefits from us. And so it is with moving beyond ex-gay relationships. The whole body of Christ can be strengthened.

Some people have identified "plateau" symptoms in their lives that have resulted from fear about where emotional healing would take them:

Luanna: "When I first became a Christian, I was afraid God would force me to get married. It was only after I got over that fear that the Lord could really begin to work in my life. Within a couple of years, I realized that I was no longer homosexual. I had reached the plateau, a place of asexual contentment.

"Now, after four more years, there has been an awakening of heterosexual feelings. To get off the plateau, you have to be willing to take risks. The way off begins with prayer."

Shawn: "A few years after coming out of homosexuality, I reached a place of comfort. I had some very satisfying same-sex friendships. I thought, *I could stay at this place for the rest of my life.* It's then I realized that something was wrong—there were no significant female friendships in my life."

Starla: "The plateau is a place where you get real content, surround yourself with people 'in the ministry,' and avoid reaching out into the church. To get off, you have to become involved with the heterosexual church scene. You have to take that risk and say, 'Doggone, I'm going to do this and like it, even if it kills me!'

"That was my attitude when my roommate and I threw a Christmas party several years ago. We invited an equal number of men and women and I was surprised what a good time I had. It was a turning point for me."[5]

Getting off this plateau of stalled growth means facing your fears, especially facing the fear of opposite-sex friendships and forming close friendships with men and women who do not have a homosexual past.

To reach maturity we have to stop avoiding the issues and relationships that have held us back. Many people have been challenged by this statement from Jeff Konrad, author of *You Don't Have to Be Gay:* "Run toward the things that frighten you. Face up to your fears. Our fears have locked us into the lies of Satan, preventing us from living and being the men and women God has created us to be."[6]

The Challenge of Singleness

We have taken a detailed look in the past several chapters at different aspects of moving toward heterosexual relationships in terms of dating, engagement and marriage. This is an appropriate place to reaffirm the validity of being single.

The majority of former homosexuals are single, even those who have been out of same-sex immorality for many years. Some left homosexuality while in their late twenties or older and simply have not found a suitable potential spouse. Others have been married previously and hesitate to initiate a new marriage. Some are content in their singleness and feel no desire to begin dating. Whatever the reason, the Bible assures us that singleness is a positive thing; it should not cause us embarrassment or shame.

The apostle Paul held up the single life as an ideal way for the Christian to serve God with a minimum of distractions. "It is good for a man not to marry. . . . I wish that all men were [single] as I am," he said (1 Cor 7:1, 7).

I (Bob) was single for the first six years of my ministry involvement at Love In Action. Looking back, I can see that I got a lot more ministry done back then than I can now as a married person. I lived in our community live-in program, so I could talk with a wide variety of people almost any hour of the day or night. Also, I was blazing with enthusiasm about being in ex-gay ministry, and I couldn't cram my enthusiasm into an eight-hour day at the office. So I would often return to work in the evenings to accomplish even more. My schedule as a single person was totally flexible; I could change my mind at a moment's notice.

Now, of course, that level of ministry involvement is simply not possible. I have a much more fixed schedule, with less spontaneity. I must reserve sufficient evenings at home to provide quality companionship for my wife. She is involved in a busy full-time career, as well as pursuing postgraduate studies, so I have numerous duties around the house in the evenings and on weekends.

Paul said that "a married man is concerned about the affairs of this world—how he can please his wife—and his interests are divided . . . [and] a married woman is concerned about the affairs of this world— how she can please her husband" (1 Cor 7:32-34). If children are present in a marriage, the duties and distractions are multiplied greatly.

A single adult may face many social pressures, even within the church. Singles hear comments like, "You're less than whole," "You're really missing out" and "What's wrong with you?"

The former homosexual who is single can also experience other pressures. Many of us know the humiliation of being confronted by church friends. "And when are you going to start thinking about marriage?" they ask. Many times it is not appropriate to give them the truth: "When I get these homosexual issues resolved in my life and God leads me to the right person, that's when!"

Other former gays or lesbians may struggle with feelings of condemnation: "I must be doing something wrong. I've been out of homosexual activities for four years. If I were *really* healed, I'd be married by now!"

Resist such condemning thoughts. Often men and women are single due to lack of opportunity for marriage—not lack of desire. Singleness is only a problem when God is leading us into a heterosexual relationship and we are resisting his will for our lives. I (Bob) know that God led me clearly and directly into a relationship that led to marriage. If I had resisted his direction, I would have been walking in disobedience.

But fourteen years ago when I came to Love In Action, my sole desire was to become the man that God created me to be. I was not concerned about marriage at that time. I enjoyed many exciting, fulfilling years as a single adult in active ministry before marriage even became an option for me. Our ultimate challenge is to live each day to the fullest, seeking to accomplish everything that God has appointed for that twenty-four-hour period. That goal applies to *every* Christian—whether single or married.

The Joy of Freedom

God desires that we all live in freedom. Free from the harmful effects of our past. Free to love him and serve him with purpose and fulfillment. What's motivating you to pursue homosexual recovery?

Jeff Konrad explains his underlying motivation in seeking freedom from homosexuality: "All I wanted was more of Jesus in my life. And more of his resurrected power in my life."

Jeff says that the transformation that God has brought about in his life is nothing short of a miracle. "Years ago, I was a shy little boy.

If I was walking down a corridor at school and saw people coming toward me, I would run around the building so I didn't have to walk by them. I would hold my head down, so I wouldn't have to have eye contact with them. I loathed myself. I felt ugly and unmanly."

Now, after pursuing homosexual recovery since 1983, Jeff feels radically different. "Today, I'm excited about life. God has made me into a man. I can look in the mirror and like who I see.

"God wants to bless us so much, but we have to open ourselves to receive what he has to give us. We can keep these shields there and prevent his love from penetrating, or we can open ourselves up and say, 'God, do your work.'

"I'm excited about what the Lord has done in my life. I never dreamed that I could be this free."[7]

Starla Allen, whose story we shared in chapter one, is also excited about the changes that God has brought about in her life. "Experiencing God's unconditional love has given me a freedom and inner strength," she says. "In the last few years, the Lord has been working with me to help me appropriate that strength. Now I can shed the tough exterior I used to have and allow myself to become vulnerable in relationships. It's exciting to realize that real strength isn't standing alone; it's being strong enough and free enough to need other people, to be open to them, able to trust them and love them."

Starla's lessons in learning to trust men have been ongoing. Years ago, while on staff with a Christian ministry at an isolated ranch, she realized one weekend that she was alone on the ranch with two other male staff members. Memories of her rape as a teenager began flooding her mind and she panicked. Finally, she said to herself, "God is going to take care of me. Whatever happens, I know that God is here with me."

Before the weekend was over, Starla and the men had shared some prayer times together. "I saw that these men had their own struggles and vulnerabilities, just like I did." Through this experience, Starla learned that men can be kind, respectful and supportive, just like her female friends. The weekend marked another small step forward in her healing process.

Today, Starla says that she stands "in awe" of the work that God has done in her life. "I am not even close to being the same person that I was years ago when I was involved in lesbianism. Back then, life was so empty that I struggled with suicidal thoughts. Now my life is full of purpose and hope for the future.

"All of this grace I owe to the gentle but firm bidding of the Holy Spirit, God's faithfulness and his unceasing love."[8]

Mike Reed's story began this book. His growth is ongoing. Several months ago an artist friend drew a picture of Mike with two of his three children. When Mike looked at the drawing, he was deeply impacted by the image. "I saw my healthy, ruddy appearance. There was confidence, peacefulness. I saw security. Manliness. The picture showed my oldest son tucked right under my arm. I was holding my little daughter. I could see the fatherly spirit and the sense of fulfillment in my face. I saw a person who had been tested and who had overcome."

Eighteen years ago Mike was in the homosexual lifestyle. "If someone had drawn a picture of me then, you would have seen just the opposite qualities. Someone who was pale and sickly, insecure and restless. Gloom was my main characteristic back then. I was lonely and afraid, cynical and hardened." Looking at the picture, Mike realized how much God has changed him. "He's changed my whole personality."

Mike says the past two decades have not been easy. "There were many years that I called my 'desert experience.' It was really dry. A lot of times, I felt like God wasn't even there. I wondered why I was going through all of this. What was God's purpose for it all?" But as Mike read the Scriptures, he saw that God often led his people into the wilderness to refine and test them, to equip them for entering into the "Promised Land" of fulfillment.

"Now, I wouldn't have my life any other way," says Mike. "Even the best side of the gay lifestyle is still far short of my life in Christ. No matter what happens, I have his purpose and direction and fulfillment.

"I know my life is still going to be hard at times. I'm still going to encounter a lot of difficulties and trials. But it's all part of growing. It's part of the process of God making you into the person he wants you to be."

May God give you strength and perseverance to pursue the same new freedom that is being discovered by Jeff, Starla and Mike—as well as thousands of other men and women who are walking ahead of you on the path to homosexual recovery.

Appendix A
Answers to Common Pro-Gay Arguments

Since the 1950s, an increasing number of churches and denominations have begun embracing a different interpretation of the Scriptures on homosexuality. In this appendix we want to present brief responses to some of the most common biblical and theological arguments heard in pro-gay religious groups when these Scriptures are discussed.

First we will examine the seven specific passages in the Bible that mention homosexuality, looking at the same time at the pro-gay arguments of these passages (stated in italics). Then we will look at the theological arguments that arise from the broader sexual ethics of the Bible.

Genesis 19:4-5 (Sodom and Gomorrah) and Judges 19:22 (Gibeah)
"But before they lay down, the men of the city, the men of Sodom, both young and old, all the people to the last man, surrounded the house; and they called to Lot, 'Where are the men who came to you tonight? Bring them out to us, so that we may know them' " (NRSV).

"While they were enjoying themselves, the men of the city, a perverse lot, surrounded the house, and started pounding on the door. They said to the old man, the master of the house, 'Bring out the man who came into your house, so that we may have intercourse with him' " (NRSV).

"God punished the people of Sodom and Gibeah for breaching the rules of hospitality, not for threatening homosexual assault." It is true that a breach of hospitality was gravely serious in that culture, but this argument does not bear close scrutiny. Much of the discussion here centers on the exact meaning of the men's demands to bring out the visitors so they could "know" them (Gen 19:5; Judg 19:22 RSV).

D. S. Bailey, in his widely quoted book *Homosexuality and the Western Christian Tradition,* argues that the men of Sodom and Gibeah asked "to know" (Hebrew *yada'*) the men in the sense of "to become acquainted with." This Hebrew word occurs 943 times in the Old Testament. In only a few cases does it refer to sexual intercourse, and then always to heterosexuality.[1]

There is a major problem with this argument: the responses to the men's demands strongly support a connotation of sexual violence. Lot protests, "No, my friends. Don't do this wicked thing" (Gen 19:7). The man in Judges 19 responds, "Don't be so vile" (v. 23). These answers seem inappropriate to protest a breach of hospitality, as opposed to rape; they certainly make no sense if the men merely wanted to become familiar with the visitors. Furthermore, Lot uses the same word, *yada',* in his next statement, "I have two daughters who have never slept with a man." Obviously the implication is sexual.

"Bailey's interpretations have been extremely influential . . . despite the fact that most biblical commentators do not agree with him," says Ronald M. Springett, professor of religion at Southern College in Collegedale, Tennessee. "Most scholars consider his interpretation to be ingenious but unconvincing since it fails to do justice to the immediate context."[2]

"Other biblical passages list the sins of Sodom, but don't mention homosexuality." Some verses mention sins like arrogance, unconcern for the poor, and encouraging evildoers (Jer 23:14; Ezek 16:49-50), but other passages link Sodom with sexual immorality, perversion and "filthy lives of lawless men" (2 Pet 2:7; Jude 7). God judged the city for a wide variety of sins, including homosexuality.

"God was judging intended rape, not loving homosexual behavior." God sent the divine visitors to confirm the city's wickedness. Long before this incident, the Bible says that "the men of Sodom were wicked and were sinning greatly against the Lord" (Gen 13:13) and that "the outcry against Sodom and Gomorrah" was "so great and their sin so grievous" that God determined to investigate it (18:20-21). So this incident was only a final confirmation of the homosexual activities already occurring. Certainly not all the previous homosexual behavior in the city was characterized by forcible rape.

However, pro-gay theologians are correct in saying that this passage does not provide a strong argument against prohibiting all homosexual acts. For further clarification we must turn to other biblical passages.

Leviticus 18:22 and 20:13 (Holiness Code)
"Do not lie with a man as one lies with a woman; that is detestable."

"If a man lies with a man as one lies with a woman, both of them have done what is detestable. They must be put to death; their blood will be on their own heads."

"Christians are no longer under the Old Testament law." Jesus Christ said he came to fulfill the law—not abolish it. "Anyone who breaks one of the least of these commandments and teaches others to do the same will be called least in the kingdom of heaven, but whoever practices and teaches these commands will be called great in the kingdom of heaven" (Mt 5:19).

This section of Leviticus includes other moral prohibitions against incest, adultery, bestiality, necrophilia and other sexual practices. "But," says professor Ronald Springett, "few Christians would be prepared to say that all of these activities are now allowed because the early church was freed from the Levitical law."[3]

"Christians break other Old Testament laws all the time, such as eating pork and lobsters. To follow some laws and break others is being grossly inconsistent." Numerous biblical scholars have pointed out the distinction between major classes of Old Testament laws. First, there are the civil and ceremonial laws, which applied only to the nation of Israel. They were specifically repealed in the New Testament (Mk 7:19; Eph 2:15; Heb 7:18; 8:13; 10:8-10). Second, there were commands that constitute the moral law, which were not limited to a certain time and place. Many of these laws—including those that apply to homosexual behavior—were repeated in the New Testament (Mt 5:27-30; Mk 7:21-23; 1 Cor 5:1; 6:9-10, 18).

Civil laws concerned such matters of daily life as borrowing of another's livestock (Ex 22:10-14), principles of restitution for lost property (Ex 22:7-9), and testifying in a lawsuit (Ex 23:1-3). Ceremonial laws defined actions or events that rendered someone unclean for ceremonial purposes, such as the handling of the dead, having any hemorrhage or emission from the body, or eating of unclean food.[4]

Then there are the moral laws. Here is how Dr. John Oswalt, professor of biblical studies at Asbury Theological Seminary in Wilmore, Kentucky, describes them: "These offenses are not related to either civil or ceremonial behavior. They do not render one unclean or require the payment of a fine. Rather these misdeeds are wrong at any time in any place. To suggest that these actions, which carry the death penalty, are of no greater significance than the eating of pork, which only renders one ceremonially unclean, betrays a serious misunderstanding of the biblical statements."[5]

"These verses forbid idolatrous homosexual practices, not homosexual behavior that has no religious overtones." Similarly, this argument says that the presence of male prostitutes in the land was condemned; their removal was accepted as a sign of spiritual reformation (1 Kings 14:24; 22:46). So God's prohibition against same-sex practices, they say, spoke of his judgment against idolatry, not against physical lovemaking by two committed homosexuals. But the context of these laws against homosexual behavior includes condemnation of intercourse with blood relations and adultery. These relationships could be every bit as tender and affectionate as the love-bond between two men or two women. But they are strictly forbidden—no matter what the context. These verses speak against certain sexual practices—including homosexuality—in all circumstances. The ban is absolute.

Romans 1:24-27

"Therefore God gave them over in the sinful desires of their hearts to sexual impurity for the degrading of their bodies with one another. They exchanged the truth of God for a lie, and worshiped and served created things rather than the Creator—who is forever praised. Amen.

"Because of this, God gave them over to shameful lusts. Even their women exchanged natural relations for unnatural ones. In the same way the men also abandoned natural relations with women and were inflamed with lust for one another. Men committed indecent acts with other men, and received in themselves the due penalty for their perversion."

"The apostle Paul's statements are 'culturally bound.' They are addressed to first-century Jews; they don't apply to us today." Under this reasoning, we can toss out the entire Bible. None of it was written to twentieth-century people. This argument implies that God's standards change from era to era. But here is what the biblical writers said: "The word of our God stands forever" (Is 40:8) and "All your words are true; all your righteous laws are eternal" (Ps 119:160).

"Paul is only condemning men and women who abandon sexual behavior that is natural to them, that is, heterosexuals who have homosexual relations. He is not condemning those who are naturally homosexual." This debate centers around the meaning of Paul's word for "natural." Professor Ronald Springett says that "Paul uses the terms *para physin* (against, beside, or contrary to nature) and *kata physin* (according to nature). These Greek words are used to express an ethical judgment on homosexuality."[6]

Other biblical scholars agree. The phrase "against nature," says Dr. Richard Lovelace, professor of church history at Gordon-Conwell Theological Seminary, "does not mean that it is against the 'natural orientation' or inner drives of an individual, for [Paul] distinctly says that the desires and actions of those mentioned in verses 26-27 are homosexual and in harmony with one another. 'Against nature' simply means against God's intention for human sexual behavior which is plainly visible in nature, in the complementary function of male and female sexual organs and temperaments."[7]

"Paul didn't understand the complexities of homosexuality as we do today. He never condemned permanent, loving homosexual relationships, just homosexual lust and promiscuity." Paul lived in a complex society, similar to our own in many ways. "New Testament authors could not have been ignorant of something so common as homosexuality in the Greco-Roman world," says Dr. J. Harold Greenlee, former professor of New Testament Greek at Asbury Theological Seminary.[8] William Barclay, a well-known New Testament scholar, says that, although homosexuality permeated Greek society, "it was regarded as abnormal, and it was never legal."[9]

Paul could have easily drawn a distinction between various forms of homosexuality if appropriate, but he condemned all homosexual behavior, with no exceptions.

1 Corinthians 6:9-10 and 1 Timothy 1:9-11

"Do you not know that the wicked will not inherit the kingdom of God? Do not be deceived: Neither the sexually immoral nor idolaters nor adulterers nor male prostitutes nor homosexual offenders nor thieves nor the greedy nor drunkards nor slanderers nor swindlers will inherit the kingdom of God."

"We also know that law is made not for good men but for lawbreakers and rebels, the ungodly and sinful, the unholy and irreligious; for those who kill their fathers or mothers, for murderers, for adulterers and perverts, for slave traders and liars and perjurers—and for whatever else is contrary to the sound doctrine that conforms to the glorious gospel of the blessed God."

"The original words in these verses refer to other forms of immorality, such as male prostitution, not to loving, permanent gay relationships." The Greek word translated "homosexual offenders" in 1 Corinthians 6:9 and "perverts" in 1 Timothy 1:10 is *arsenokoites*. Thayer's Greek-English Lexicon (1885) translates this word as "one who lies with a male as with a female, a sodomite." Bauer, Arndt and Gingrich's lexicon (1957) translates it as "a male homosexual, pederast, sodomite," the same meaning which occurs in ancient Greek writings such as *Anthologia Palatina* and the *Catalogus Codicum Astrologorum Graecorum.*[10] The word is derived from *arsen,* "a male" and *koite,* "a bed." With the suffix *-tes* indicating the person performing the action, the etymology of the word is "a male-bed-person."

"It is clear, then," says Dr. Harold Greenlee, "that an *arsenokoites* in the New Testament is a man who goes to bed with a male for sexual purposes. This has been its accepted meaning ever since the time of ancient Greek literature."[11] In this passage Paul is broadly condemning all homosexual acts, not just prostitution. "If Paul was condemning only one kind of homosexual activity here, and by implication allowing others, he surely would have been more explicit," agrees Ronald Springett.[12]

Theological Arguments

Besides specific verses on homosexuality, the biblical perspective on this type of behavior must be looked at in a broader context of biblical teachings on sexuality as a whole.

"Jesus didn't speak against homosexuality." There are several points to make in response to this common argument. First, the Bible does not mention Jesus' statements on other forms of sexual behavior, such as incest, rape, child abuse and bestiality. Few would argue that, therefore, these behaviors are permissible. The Bible says that many things Jesus said were not recorded (Jn 21:25). So he could have mentioned homosexuality, although he probably had no occasion to do so. The Jews of his day were strictly opposed to such practices.

Jesus upheld the Old Testament laws on sexual behavior (Mt 5:27-30; Mk 7:21-23), which strongly condemned homosexual acts. And Jesus only spoke of sexuality in the context of a lifelong heterosexual commitment, when he mentioned the creation of male and female (Mt 19:4-9).

This reference back to the creation account is most significant. The Bible's perspective on sexual expression is consistent throughout the Scriptures. Richard F. Lovelace says that pro-gay theologians often dismiss certain verses on homosexuality but "usually fail to deal theologically with the subject in terms of the Bible's general teaching on human sexuality."[13]

"The starting point," Lovelace continues, "for understanding both human sexuality in general and homosexuality should be the account of the creation of man and woman in Genesis 1 and 2."[14]

Lovelace notes that the creation account emphasizes how humanity was created in God's image as male and female. To remedy Adam's "aloneness," the Lord did not create another man, but a woman. This suggests that male and female are complementary not just sexually, but also in other ways, such as emotionally and socially.

God blessed the man and woman, and then gave them his first command: "Be fruitful and increase in number" (Gen 1:28). The first woman was physically crafted from the flesh of the man (2:21-22). When they united physically, they became "one flesh" again (2:24). "Heterosexual intercourse in marriage is more than a union," says theologian John R. W. Stott. "It is a kind of reunion. It is not a union of alien persons who do not belong to one another and cannot appropriately become one flesh. On the contrary, it is the union of two persons who originally were one, were then separated from each other, and now in the sexual encounter of marriage come together again."[15]

Each sexual union of husband and wife is a powerful reminder of God's created order. "It is no accident therefore," Lovelace says, "that every form of sexual expression outside the marriage covenant which is the center of the family is explicitly or implicitly condemned in the remainder of Scripture."[16]

Jesus himself directly referred back to Genesis 2:24 in teaching that marriage should be a permanent relationship between a man and a woman; he presented celibacy as the only approved sexual lifestyle apart from heterosexual marriage (Mt 19:4-12). In one sermon, Jesus condemned "sexual immorality" (Mk 7:21). The Greek word he used was *porneia*, which includes any form of sexual behavior outside of heterosexual marriage.

"Jesus spoke of a higher law of love, and faithful long-term homosexual relationships can be just as loving as heterosexual marriages." This argument centers around a discussion of what is meant by the word *love*. If we define Christian love in terms of self-giving, it is true that some homosexual relationships are more loving than some heterosexual marriages.

But, despite the stress that Jesus laid on the necessity of a loving motive, nowhere did he teach that a motive of love can justify anything. He never gave his disciples any reason to believe that, because of his teaching on love, they could ignore the Old Testament laws which labeled some things as bad in themselves, whatever the motive (see Mt 5:17-20). Jesus said that his love was reflected by our obedience to his commandments (Jn 14:15).

Replacing all other absolute standards by the single command to love is not only unfaithful to New Testament teaching, it is also totally inadequate as a guide for moral living. Self-deception and external influences blur everyone's vision at times, especially in the context of expressing our sexual desires.

Some Final Thoughts

If someone tries to support homosexual behavior from Scripture, look up the verse in several translations, and study the context of the whole passage. For example, some have said that this verse supports homosexuality: "Do not allow what you consider good to be spoken of as evil" (Rom 14:16). But the context is speaking of the Old Testament dietary laws. Paul is discussing clean and unclean foods—not pure or impure moral practices.

The Bible never speaks positively about homosexuality or any other sexual practices outside a lifelong heterosexual commitment. Difficult as this standard is to obey, it is the calling of Christ for *all* his followers, including those with same-sex attractions and desires.

For further study on this important subject, see the "Pro-Gay Theology" section of appendix B. Some of the responses to the questions in this appendix have been adapted from David Field's *The Homosexual Way—A Christian Option?* (InterVarsity Press, 1979).

Appendix B
For Further Reading

Overcoming Homosexuality

Comiskey, Andrew. *Pursuing Sexual Wholeness.* Lake Mary, Fla.: Creation House, 1989. An ex-gay shares principles of freedom from homosexuality.

Consiglio, William. *Homosexual No More.* Wheaton, Ill.: Victor Books, 1991. Practical strategies by a psychologist.

Dallas, Joe. *Desires in Conflict.* Eugene, Ore.: Harvest House, 1991. A helpful book on overcoming homosexuality, especially for men.

Howard, Jeanette. *Out of Egypt.* Tunbridge Wells, England: Monarch, 1991. A very helpful book for women, written by a former lesbian. Available in North America through Regeneration Books, P.O. Box 9830, Baltimore, MD 21284.

Konrad, Jeff. *You Don't Have to Be Gay.* Hilo, Hawaii: Pacific Publishing, 1992. An ex-gay gives practical help in overcoming homosexuality. Available through Regeneration Books, P.O. Box 9830, Baltimore, MD 21284.

Moberly, Elizabeth R. *Homosexuality: A New Christian Ethic.* Greenwood, S.C.: Attic Press, 1983. Very helpful reading on homosexual causation, especially the crucial role of disruption in parent-child bonding.

Payne, Leanne. *The Broken Image.* Westchester, Ill.: Crossway Books, 1981. An important book for understanding the role of prayer in homosexual healing.

Saia, Michael R. *Counseling the Homosexual.* Minneapolis: Bethany House, 1988. Although written for pastors and counselors, contains many good insights for the ex-gay reader.

Homosexuality and Marriage

Baker, Don. *Beyond Rejection.* Portland, Ore.: Multnomah, 1985. Testimony of a married man's struggle with homosexuality.

Parent-Child Issues

Coleman, William. *How to Go Home Without Feeling Like a Child.* Dallas: Word, 1991. Resolving problems between grown children and their parents.

Frank, Maureen. *Dealing with the Dad of Your Past.* Minneapolis: Bethany House, 1990. Resolving daughter-father issues.

Love, Patricia, with Jo Robinson. *The Emotional Incest Syndrome.* New York: Bantam, 1990. A secular book dealing with an overly intimate parent-child relationship. Especially helpful for sons with "smother mothers."

Smalley, Gary, and John Trent. *The Blessing.* Nashville: Thomas Nelson, 1986. Includes an important section for adults on repairing relationships with their parents.

Strom, Kay Marshall. *Making Friends with Your Father.* Grand Rapids: Zondervan, 1992. A book for daughters.

Williams, Charles. *Forever a Father, Always a Son.* Wheaton, Ill.: Victor Books, 1991. Explores the father-son relationship and gives guidance on how to repair it.

Engagement

Smith, M. Blaine. *Should I Get Married?* Downers Grove, Ill.: InterVarsity Press, 1990. Crucial reading for making the big decision.

Wright, H. Norman. *So You're Getting Married.* Ventura, Calif.: Regal, 1985. Covers all the basics for engaged couples.

Marriage (General)

Dobson, James. *What Wives Wish Their Husbands Knew About Women.* Wheaton, Ill.: Tyndale, 1975. Helpful for men who want to meet their wife's emotional needs.

Drescher, John, and Betty Drescher. *If We Were Starting Our Marriage Again.* Nashville: Abingdon, 1985. Thought-provoking reading for engaged and newly married couples.

Frank, Don, and Jan Frank. *When Victims Marry.* San Bernardino, Calif.: Here's Life, 1990. Help for married couples in overcoming the effects of childhood abuse.

Hart, Kathleen Fischer, and Thomas N. Hart. *The First Two Years of Marriage.* New York: Paulist Press, 1983. Excellent for newlyweds.

Hybels, Bill, and Lynne Hybels. *Fit to Be Tied.* Grand Rapids: Zondervan, 1991. Helpful principles interwoven with testimony of a pastor and his wife who had numerous incompatibilities to resolve—excellent.

Rainey, Barbara, and Dennis Rainey. *Building Your Mate's Self-Esteem.* San Bernardino, Calif.: Here's Life, 1986. Helpful reading for spouses of those with emotional issues from the past.

Sexuality in Marriage

Ells, Alfred. *Restoring Innocence.* Nashville: Thomas Nelson, 1990. Dealing with past memories which are hurting your marital intimacy.

Penner, Clifford, and Joyce Penner. *The Gift of Sex.* Dallas: Word, 1981. An excellent guide to a more satisfying sexual life in marriage. (Unfortunately, the authors state that those troubled by homosexuality rarely achieve satisfying marriages. Ignore them on this point!)

Wheat, Ed, and Gaye Wheat. *Intended for Pleasure.* Old Tappan, N.J.: Fleming H. Revell, 1981. Detailed advice on attaining a satisfying sexual life in marriage.

Troubled Marriages

Carter, Les. *The Prodigal Spouse.* Nashville: Thomas Nelson, 1990. Dealing with adultery.

Rosenau, Douglas. *Slaying the Marriage Dragons.* Wheaton, Ill.: Victor, 1991. Building a stronger marriage relationship.

Talley, Jim. *Reconcilable Differences.* Nashville: Thomas Nelson, 1991. For separated or divorced couples who want to repair their relationship.

Virkler, Henry A. *Broken Promises.* Dallas: Word, 1992. Dealing with adultery.

Williams, Pat, and Jill Williams with Jerry Jenkins. *Rekindled.* Old Tappan, N.J.: Fleming H. Revell, 1985. The story of one marriage that almost died and how it was revived.

Incest/Sexual Abuse

Allender, Dan B. *The Wounded Heart.* Colorado Springs: NavPress, 1990. A penetrating look at the deeper issues arising from sexual abuse.

Buhler, Rich. *Pain and Pretending.* Nashville: Thomas Nelson, 1988. Helpful insights for the victim of past sexual abuse. Includes some male abuse anecdotes.

Frank, Jan. *A Door of Hope.* San Bernardino, Calif.: Here's Life, 1987. Practical step-by-step guide on dealing with incest, written by a survivor.

Lew, Mike. *Victims No Longer.* New York: Harper & Row, 1988, 1990. A secular book for men who have been sexually abused.

Talley, Jim A., and Jane Carlile Baker. *My Father's Love.* San Bernardino, Calif.: Here's Life, 1992. Testimony of a woman overcoming sexual abuse.

Walters, Candace L. *Invisible Wounds: What Every Woman Should Know About Sexual Assault.* Portland, Ore.: Multnomah, 1987, 1988. Helpful reading for women who have been raped.

Sexual Addiction

Arterburn, Steve. *Addicted to "Love."* Ann Arbor, Mich.: Servant Publications, 1991. Overcoming unhealthy dependencies in romance, relationships and sex.

Carnes, Patrick. *Don't Call It Love.* New York: Bantam, 1991. Helpful insights on overcoming sexual addiction from a secular perspective.

Carnes, Patrick. *Out of the Shadows.* Minneapolis: CompCare Publishers, 1983. The classic secular book on overcoming sexual addiction.

Schaumburg, Harry, *False Intimacy.* Colorado Springs: NavPress, 1992. An excellent book on the biblical solution to sexual addiction.

HIV/AIDS

Jarvis, Debra. *HIV Positive.* Batavia, Ill.: Lion, 1990. Working through the emotions of living with HIV disease.

Perry, Shireen, with Gregg Lewis. *In Sickness and in Health.* Downers Grove, Ill.: InterVarsity Press, 1989. Eye-opening account of a married couple whose marriage is invaded by AIDS.

Friendships/Relationships

Inrig, Gary. *Quality Friendship.* Chicago: Moody Press, 1981. Basic principles of forming significant relationships.

Rentzel, Lori. *Emotional Dependency.* Downers Grove, Ill.: InterVarsity Press, 1991. Helpful insights when a friendship becomes too emotionally enmeshed.

Smith, David W. *Men Without Friends.* Nashville: Thomas Nelson, 1990. Help for men in developing meaningful same-sex friendships.

Countering Pro-Gay Theology

Lanning, Cynthia, ed. *Answers to Your Questions About Homosexuality.* Wilmore, Ky.: Bristol Books, 1988. Includes a chapter on Old Testament passages and another chapter on New Testament teachings.

Stott, John. *Homosexual Partnerships? Why Same-Sex Relationships Are Not a Christian Option.* Downers Grove, Ill.: InterVarsity Press, 1984, 1985. A booklet which includes a brief but concise discussion of pertinent passages.

Yamamoto, J. Isamu, ed. *The Crisis of Homosexuality.* Wheaton, Ill.: Victor Books, 1990. Includes a chapter on Old Testament texts and a chapter on the New Testament teachings regarding homosexuality.

Appendix C
Resources for Additional Help

Local Support Groups

Exodus International is a coalition of Christian ministries worldwide that offer support to men and women seeking to overcome homosexuality. These outreaches offer such services as support groups, one-on-one counseling, literature, newsletters and other helpful resources. For a free introductory packet of literature on Exodus, including a complete list of referral ministries, contact Exodus International, P.O. Box 2121, San Rafael, CA 94912; 415/454-1017.

Audiotapes

Each year Exodus International hosts a national conference on overcoming homosexuality. Dozens of workshops are professionally audiotaped, covering such subjects as ex-gay men's issues, ex-lesbian issues, help for friends and family members, counseling problems, and dealing with AIDS. For a free tape catalog and order form, contact Exodus International, P.O. Box 2121, San Rafael, CA 94912; 415/454-1017.

Books

There are numerous excellent books on different aspects of overcoming homosexuality and lesbianism. Most of them are available through your local Christian bookstore (see appendix B for details of suggested titles). If you prefer, you can conveniently obtain many of these books by mail order. For a free catalog of books on homosexuality and related issues, contact Regeneration Books, P.O. Box 9830, Baltimore, MD 21284; 410/661-0284.

Appendix D
Questions for Individuals or Groups

Chapter 1: Can Homosexuals Really Change?
1. What does change mean to you?

2. Do you believe change is possible for men and women from a homosexual background? to what extent?

3. How does the Bible describe change (see 1 Corinthians 6)?

4. What changes have you already experienced as a result of your relationship with Christ?

5. What areas, to you, seem unaltered by your experience as a Christian?

6. What was your reaction to the stories presented in this chapter? (Did they seem believable or unbelievable to you?) Explain.

7. What are some areas of change you'd like to see and, with God's help, experience in your own life? Discuss and/or write your response in a journal.

Chapter 2: Biblical and Scientific Evidence for Change
1. This chapter talks about coming to terms with the Bible's position on homosexuality. What has been your own journey in resolving this issue? (For example, were you raised as a Christian and "always believed it was wrong" but struggled with same-sex attractions? Or did you become a Christian later in life and subsequently considered the position of Scripture on homosexual issues?)

2. What conclusions, if any, have you reached about pro-gay interpretations of Scripture?

3. How do your feelings about the Bible's statements on homosexuality affect your feelings toward God?

4. For women, how do you respond to statements from the Bible on women and women's roles?

5. How do we balance trust in God with any unresolved feelings we may have?

6. Why is heterosexuality a poor goal for Christians coming out of a homosexual background?

What are some well-placed goals for us as we grow in our understanding of God and of ourselves?

Chapter 3: The Dynamics of Change

1. Whether you're investigating Christianity for the first time, renewing a childhood commitment or seeking to strengthen and deepen your relationship with Christ, reflect on where you've been and what has brought you to this point. Where are you in your Christian journey?

2. What does the concept of the "lordship of Christ" mean to you?

How does this concept relate to your sexuality?

3. Review the section of this chapter called "Avenues of Change." Which of these disciplines are currently a part of your life?

Which ones would you like to develop further?

4. Have you been able to share with others about your homosexual struggles? If not, consider opening up to at least one trusted individual who could support you with prayer and concern.

Chapter 4: Exposing the Roots

1. When did you first begin to question your sexual identity?

2. From your reading, how would you compare the roots of male homosexuality with the roots of lesbianism?

3. How does this chapter relate to your own life story? Referring to the list on page 43, journal about or discuss with a group how you were affected by early childhood development, family background, temperament, peer pressure and/or sexual abuse.

4. In prayer either alone or with prayer partners seek God's wisdom and healing regarding the past events in your life that have been hurtful. Such healing may take months, or even years, so be patient.

Chapter 5: Saying Goodby

1. Recall your own decision to "come out" of the homosexual lifestyle (or your current feelings, if you are now contemplating such a decision). What factors are motivating you to leave homosexuality behind?

2. What aspects of this decision are especially painful for you? Identify these areas, pray about them and talk about them with a group or individual you trust.

What practical things can you do to help with each area of struggle?

3. Have you experienced grief as a part of your decision to leave the lifestyle? Explain.

Explore other resources on grief at your local library or bookstore. Understanding this process can bring tremendous relief.

4. What do you think is the most difficult part of ending a gay or lesbian relationship?

5. Describe some ways, both healthy and unhealthy, you've dealt with loneliness.

6. Have you been tested for HIV? Why or why not?

Chapter 6: Breaking Addictive Patterns

1. The authors, on page 68, make two statements: "Our homosexual and lesbian feelings point to deeper emotional needs," and later, "Therefore these needs can potentially be met through nonsexual relationships." Read these statements and the paragraphs that surround them. Discuss or journal about your own feelings and beliefs regarding these statements, particularly as they pertain to your own life experiences.

2. What role, if any, has pornography played in your struggles?

3. When do you believe a sexual temptation evolves into sin?

4. What are your most effective strategies for dealing with sexual temptation?

5. Have you ever gotten rid of a personal or household item that seemed to tie you to your past lifestyle? What effect, if any, did this have on your spiritual growth?

Chapter 7: What's On Your Mind?

1. Make a list of those things which are your "triggers" to sexual temptation. Examples might include certain times of day, physical conditions such as fatigue, emotions such as anger or sadness.

2. How can you better deal with these "triggers"?

3. Read Ephesians 6:10-18. List the weapons of spiritual warfare described there, applying each specifically to your own struggles.

4. Think of books, music, art or films that have given you hope and inspiration. Which ones have had a deep, positive impact on your spiritual and emotional life?

5. The final section of this chapter, "Getting Proper Support," lists several avenues of help for people seeking to overcome homosexual struggles. Which of these have you found helpful?

How might you make use of the options you have not yet explored?

Chapter 8: Change in Self-Identity

1. What do you think of the concept of giving up not only homosexual acts, but identity as well?

Is such a goal desirable, or even possible? Explain.

2. Do you agree with the statement "Everyone is born heterosexual"? Why or why not?

3. How would you identify yourself today in terms of gender identity?

4. List a few Bible characters who you might consider as role models. What qualities do you admire in those you've listed?

Chapter 9: Forming Healthy Friendships

1. What has been your greatest hindrance in forming healthy friendships?

2. Do you tend toward emotional dependency, defensive detachment or both?

3. Using the list on page 112, identify ways you've experienced manipulation by others or have used manipulative tactics in relationships yourself.

4. What character qualities do you look for in a friend?

5. If you've experienced a close friendship with someone who doesn't fit your usual "type," describe ways that relationship impacted your life.

Chapter 10: Making Peace with Your Abusive Past

1. List three ways that past abuse (whether sexual, verbal or emotional) leads to adult homosexual struggles.

2. Of the five self-accusations listed on pages 127-29, with which do you identify most strongly?

3. If you can remember making an inner vow at any time in your past, write down that vow. Is that vow still affecting your life in any way?

4. Have you ever confronted a past abuser with their mistreatment of you? If so, describe any results that came from this encounter.

Chapter 11: Dating and Romance

1. Describe the most significant opposite sex relationship you've experienced (other than with a family member).

In what ways did that relationship affect your life?

2. What are some guidelines for keeping opposite-sex friendships healthy?

3. How might you guard against misunderstandings of the type Bob describes in the beginning of the chapter?

4. What are some possible indicators that a former homosexual or lesbian is ready to begin dating?

5. As healing in your life progresses, describe changes and growth you observe in your relationships with the opposite sex.

In what areas would you like to see more progress?

Chapter 12: Getting Ready for Marriage

1. What are your greatest fears about marriage?

2. Do you believe HIV-positive individuals should consider marriage? Why or why not?

3. How important is sexual attraction in considering a potential marriage partner?

What other factors are important to you?

4. If marriage is a future prospect for you, write down your hopes and visions for a marriage relationship.

5. What growth and goals can you pursue now to prepare yourself for such a relationship?

Chapter 13: Growing in Marital Intimacy

1. List the three most significant reasons you got married.

2. What do you consider to be the greatest strength of your marriage? the greatest weakness?

3. How freely do you talk with your spouse regarding your struggles and sexual temptations? (If you don't feel free to share with your spouse, do you have an "accountability partner" with whom you can talk?)

4. Do you find that being married helps you to resist or overcome sexual temptations? If so, how?

4. In what ways, if any, does marriage add to your pressures and temptations?

Discuss or journal about ways you might deal with such pressures more effectively.

5. If you could begin your marriage again, what would you do differently?

Chapter 14: A Vision for the Future

1. How do you feel about the label "ex-gay"?

2. Where would you like to be in terms of your sexual healing one year from now? in five years? in ten years?

3. Do you envision yourself talking about your gay or lesbian background in the future? For example, you might give a public testimony or counsel others who are struggling.

Even if you prefer to keep your background private, pray about ways to use your healing experience to help others.

Notes

Chapter 1: Can Homosexuals Really Change?
[1]For simplicity's sake the authors have chosen to use the terms *straight* for men or women who have never struggled with homosexuality and *former homosexual (ex-gay, ex-lesbian,* etc.) for those who have experienced this struggle, even if the latter are now predominantly or exclusively heterosexual in thoughts, feelings, identity and/or actions.

[2]Some material was taken from Starla Allen, "Releasing the Woman Within," in *Pursuing Sexual Wholeness Guide* (Lake Mary, Fla.: Creation House, 1988), pp. 172-74. Used by permission.

Chapter 2: Biblical and Psychological Evidence for Change
[1]If you wish to do more study on these passages concerning homosexuality, there are excellent resources available on this subject, such as John Stott, *Homosexual Partnerships?* (Downers Grove, Ill.: InterVarsity Press, 1985) and J. Isamu Yamamoto, ed., *The Crisis of Homosexuality* (Wheaton, Ill.: Victor Books, 1990), chaps. 9-10. See also appendix A for answers to specific pro-gay arguments on these biblical passages.

[2]*The Teaching of the Twelve Apostles* 2.2, cited by David D. Bundy, *What You Should Know About Homosexuality,* ed. Charles W. Keysor (Grand Rapids: Zondervan, 1979), p. 120.

[3]Simon LeVay, "A Difference in Hypothalamic Structure Between Heterosexual and Homosexual Men," *Science* 253 (Aug. 1991): 1034-37.

[4]Ibid., p. 1036.

[5]Sharon Begley with David Gelman, "What Causes People to Be Homosexual?" *Newsweek,* Sept. 9, 1991, p. 52.

[6]Anne Fausto-Sterling, professor of medical science at Brown University, as quoted in *Time,* Sept. 9, 1991, p. 61.

[7]Kathy Tait, "Homosexuality: Born or Bred?" *The Province* (Vancouver, B.C.), Mar. 23, 1992, p. C7.

[8]There was another curious result in this study. Of the twenty-seven iden-

tical twins who were not concordant (i.e. homosexual-heterosexual pairs), twenty-one of the heterosexuals scored a Kinsey scale 0 (the homosexual member was 6). One would expect a strong genetic factor to yield many more results in the Kinsey 3-4 range. (Thanks to Dr. Neil Whitehead, New Zealand, for providing this important insight in personal correspondence with the authors, Jan. 20, 1993.)

[9]Reuben Fine, "Psychoanalytic Theory," in *Male and Female Homosexuality: Psychological Approaches,* ed. Louis Diamant (New York: Hemisphere, 1987), pp. 84-86.

[10]William H. Masters and Virginia E. Johnson, *Homosexuality in Perspective* (New York: Bantam, 1979), p. 400.

[11]Ibid., p. 251.

[12]Charles W. Socarides, "Homosexuality," in *American Handbook of Psychiatry,* ed. Silvano Arieti and Eugene B. Brody, 2d ed. (New York: Basic Books, 1974), 3:309.

[13]Irving Bieber, *Homosexuality: A Psychoanalytic Study* (New York: Basic Books, 1962), pp. 318-19.

[14]Irving Bieber and Toby Bieber, "Male Homosexuality," *Canadian Journal of Psychiatry* 24, no. 5 (1979): 416.

Chapter 3: The Dynamics of Change

[1]C. S. Lewis, *Mere Christianity* (New York: Macmillan, 1952), p. 44.

[2]Leanne Payne, *The Broken Image: Restoring Personal Wholeness Through Healing Prayer* (Westchester, Ill.: Good News, Crossway Books, 1981), p. 150.

[3]Adapted from Jeanette Howard, *Out of Egypt: Leaving Lesbianism Behind* (Speldhurst, Kent, England: Monarch, 1991), p. 232.

[4]There are excellent study Bibles available which will help you with this principle of application. We especially recommend the Life Application Bible and the Life Recovery Bible.

[5]For example, Ronald Klug, *How to Keep a Spiritual Journal* (Minneapolis: Augsburg, 1993).

[6]Jeff Konrad, *You Don't Have to Be Gay* (Hilo, Hawaii: Pacific House, 1992), pp. 57-59; available from Regeneration Books, P.O. Box 9830, Baltimore, MD 21284.

[7]Adapted from the article "Overcoming Fears of Relating to Men" by John Smid (Love In Action, P.O. Box 2655, San Rafael, CA 94912). Used by permission.

Chapter 4: Exposing the Roots

[1]Erik Erikson, *Childhood and Society* (New York: Norton, 1950, 1963), p. 249.

[2]Leanne Payne, *The Broken Image* (Westchester, Ill.: Good News, Crossway Books, 1981) pp. 121-136.

[3]This important subject is thoroughly explained in Elizabeth R. Moberly, *Homosexuality: A New Christian Ethic* (Cambridge, England: James Clarke

& Co., 1983).

[4]Erikson, *Childhood and Society,* p. 249.

[5]George Rekers, *Growing Up Straight* (Chicago: Moody Press, 1982), p. 73.

Chapter 6: Breaking Addictive Patterns

[1]William Consiglio, *Homosexual No More* (Wheaton, Ill.: Victor Books, 1991), p. 36.

[2]Some concepts in this section are taken from the audiotape "Fetishes, Partialisms and Fantasy" by Frank Worthen (Exodus International, 1992).

[3]Some examples are taken from Michael Saia, *Counseling the Homosexual* (Minneapolis: Bethany House, 1988), pp. 136-37.

[4]The most common Scripture used to condemn masturbation is Genesis 38:9, when Onan "spilled his semen on the ground." But this passage is talking about coitus interruptus, a method of birth control when, during sexual intercourse, a man withdraws his penis before orgasm to avoid impregnating his female partner. In Onan's case he was rebelling against the Lord's command to impregnate his brother's widow in order to raise up heirs on behalf of his deceased brother. This duty was expected in ancient Israel under their leviratic law of inheritance. When Onan disobeyed this cultural law, the Bible condemned his actions as wicked. But his behavior had nothing to do with masturbation.

[5]Some ideas in this section are taken from the audiotape "Overcoming Masturbation" by Starla Allen (Exodus International, 1992).

[6]Harvey B. Milkman and Stanley Sunderwirth, *Craving for Ecstasy: The Consciousness and Chemistry of Escape* (New York: Lexington Books, 1987), pp. 95-97, 104.

Chapter 7: What's on Your Mind?

[1]Adapted from "The War Within Continues," *Leadership,* Winter 1988, p. 28.

[2]Some ideas in this section are taken from the audiotape "Men Who Never Acted Out" by Brad Sargent (Exodus International, 1992).

Chapter 8: Change in Self-Identity

[1]Many people say, "I've had gay feelings all my life—even back to the age of three or four." We do not agree that those feelings were really an expression of a person's sexuality. The pull toward others of your own gender resulted from legitimate *emotional* needs for same-sex affirmation, not the desire to have sex with that person.

[2]Jeanette Howard, *Out of Egypt* (Speldhurst, Kent, England: Monarch Publications, 1991), p. 177.

[3]Ibid., p. 178.

[4]Some of the key ideas in this section are taken from the audiotape "Masculinity" by Alan Medinger (Exodus International, 1985).

[5]Two examples of such novels are *He Who Wept: An Epic Novel of Jeremiah* and *Daniel: The Man Who Saw Tomorrow,* both by Thom Lemmons (Sisters,

Ore.: Questar Publishers, 1991).

Chapter 9: Forming Healthy Friendships

[1]Lori Rentzel, *Emotional Dependency* (Downers Grove, Ill.: InterVarsity Press, 1990), p. 7.

[2]Ibid., pp. 8-9.

[3]Henri J. M. Nouwen, *Reaching Out* (Garden City, N.Y.: Doubleday, 1975), p. 30.

Chapter 10: Making Peace with Your Abusive Past

[1]J. Isamu Yamamoto, ed., *The Crisis of Homosexuality* (Wheaton, Ill.: Victor Books, 1990), p. 30.

[2]Mike Lew, *Victims No Longer: Men Recovering from Incest and Other Sexual Child Abuse* (New York: Harper & Row, 1988, 1990), p. 41.

[3]D. Finkelhor, as cited in Frank G. Bolton Jr., Larry A. Morris and Ann E. MacEachron, *Males at Risk: The Other Side of Child Sexual Abuse* (Newbury Park, Calif.: Sage Publications, 1989), p. 86.

[4]Adapted from Paula Sandford, *Healing Victims of Sexual Abuse* (Tulsa, Okla.: Victory House, 1988), pp. 28-41; and John and Paula Sandford, *Healing the Wounded Spirit* (South Plainfield, N.J.: Bridge Publishing, 1985), pp. 100-102.

[5]Connie Haney, "Out of Bondage," *Covenant* 1, no. 2: 2. (New Direction for Life Ministries, Box 1078, Stn F, Toronto, Ontario, Canada M4Y 2T7.) Used by permission.

[6]Howard Milton, "Ministry to the Male Incest Survivor" (Exodus International, 1991). Some of the ideas in this section are taken from this audiotape.

[7]Melinda Reinicke, "Adults Molested as Children: Resolving Self-Blame" (Exodus International, 1992).

[8]Grace H. Ketterman, *Verbal Abuse* (Ann Arbor, Mich.: Servant, 1992).

[9]Ibid., pp. 35-36.

[10]Adapted from Cynthia A. Kubetin and James Mallory, *Beyond the Darkness* (Dallas: Word Books, 1992), pp. 123-24. Used by permission.

[11]Lynda D. Elliott and Vicki L. Tanner, *My Father's Child* (Brentwood, Tenn.: Wolgemuth and Hyatt, 1988, 1991), pp. 50-52.

[12]Kubetin and Mallory, *Beyond the Darkness,* p. 166.

[13]Examples taken from the audiotape "Healing Damaged Views of Masculinity" by Janine Puls (Exodus International, 1990).

Chapter 11: Dating and Romance

[1]See for example, William L. Coleman, *Cupid Is Stupid!* (Downers Grove, Ill.: InterVarsity Press, 1991), and Tim Timmons and Charlie Hedges, *Call It Love or Call It Quits* (Dallas: Word Books, 1988). We also recommend books that give practical advice on honoring the opposite sex in all your relationships, such as Charlie W. Shedd's two books, *Letters to Karen* (New York:

Avon, 1976) and *Letters to Philip* (Old Tappan, N.J.: Revell, 1969).

[2]Some material in this chapter is taken from a lecture on dating given by John Paulk to the Love In Action (San Rafael, Calif.) live-in program, Nov. 1991.

[3]R. Paul Stevens, *Getting Ready for a Great Marriage* (Colorado Springs: NavPress, 1990), p. 73.

[4]"Ex-Lesbians and Ex-Homosexual Men: Why and When You Should Take the HIV Antibody Test" by Brad Sargent is a helpful handout explaining behaviors which expose both men and women to risk of HIV infection. For a copy, contact The Barnabas Center, P.O. Box 3875, San Rafael, CA 94912.

[5]Margaret A. Fischl et al., "Heterosexual Transmission of Human Immunodeficiency Virus (HIV): Relationship of Sexual Practices to Seroconversion," Third International Conference on AIDS, June 1-5, 1987, *Abstracts Volume*, p. 178, as cited in "In Defense of a Little Virginity," *Focus on the Family*, 1992.

[6]Ross and his wife also used the spermicidal cream nonoxynol 9. However, contrary to prior evidence, one 1992 study showed that nonoxynol 9 *increased* the transmission of HIV infection. (Joan Kreiss et al., "Efficacy of Nonoxynol 9 Contraceptive Sponge Use in Preventing Heterosexual Acquisition of HIV in Nairobi Prostitutes," *Journal of the American Medical Association*, July 22/29, 1993, pp. 477-82.) Further studies may confirm this finding. *Therefore, it is essential that readers get up-to-date medical information from their doctors before entering into sexual activities with an HIV-infected spouse.* Also, numerous secular books are available that give helpful information on precautions that can reduce the risk of infection.

[7]We could find few resources available for the HIV-positive person who is entering into dating and/or marriage. Most material for married men, for example, assumes that you were infected after marriage or entered into marriage without knowing your HIV-positive status. Contact the Christian AIDS Services Alliance (P.O. Box 3612, San Rafael, CA 94912) for a list of current resources on this issue.

Chapter 12: Getting Ready for Marriage

[1]See for example, chapter 20, "Understanding the Fear of Commitment," in M. Blaine Smith, *Should I Get Married?* (Downers Grove, Ill.: InterVarsity Press, 1990), p. 191.

[2]Columns by Ann Landers, as published in the *Chicago Sun-Times*, Jan. 14, 15, 1985.

[3]James C. Dobson, *What Wives Wish Their Husbands Knew About Women* (Wheaton, Ill.: Tyndale, 1975), p. 116, Dobson's italics.

[4]Ibid., p. 129.

[5]R. Paul Stevens, *Getting Ready for a Great Marriage* (Colorado Springs: NavPress, 1990), p. 74.

[6]Such as Ed Wheat and Gaye Wheat, *Intended for Pleasure* (Old Tappan, N.J.: Revell, 1981), or Clifford Penner and Joyce Penner, *The Gift of Sex*

(Dallas: Word Books, 1981).

[7]Kathleen Fischer Hart and Thomas N. Hart, *The First Two Years of Marriage* (Ramsey, N.J.: Paulist Press, 1983), p. 81.

[8]These same emotions which can tempt the ex-gay male to pursue homosexual adultery are identical to the emotions that tempt straight men to commit heterosexual adultery. See Henry A. Virkler, *Broken Promises* (Dallas: Word Books, 1992), p. 25.

[9]Doug Fields, *Creative Romance* (Eugene, Ore.: Harvest House, 1991), p. 9.

[10]Dobson, *What Wives Wish,* p. 89.

[11]Hart and Hart, *The First Two Years,* p. 13.

[12]Dobson, *What Wives Wish,* p. 92.

[13]In an informal survey of married ex-gay men, only one in fourteen reported being sexually aroused by sight alone. Alan P. Medinger, "Visual Stimulation and Healing," *Regeneration News,* Feb. 1992, p. 1 (P.O. Box 9830, Baltimore, MD 21284). Quotations in this section are taken from this article. Used by permission.

Chapter 13: Growing in Marital Intimacy

[1]Adapted from *Outpost News,* Jan. 1992 (published by Outpost, P.O. Box 7067, Minneapolis, MN 55407). Used by permission.

[2]R. Paul Stevens, *Getting Ready for a Great Marriage* (Colorado Springs: NavPress, 1990), p. 24.

[3]Adapted from Barbara Trump, *Forgiven Love* (Edina, Minn.: Jeremy Books, 1979), pp. 32-34.

[4]Some key ideas and quotations in this section are adapted from the article "For the Married Man Struggling with Homosexuality" by Alan Medinger (published by Regeneration, P.O. Box 9830, Baltimore, MD 21284). Used by permission.

[5]Adapted from the testimony "Beckie to Rebecca" by Rebecca Anne (Baeder) Johnston (published by Metanoia Ministries, P.O. Box 33039, Seattle, WA 98133). Used by permission.

[6]Richard Brzeczek and Elizabeth Brzeczek, *Addicted to Adultery* (New York: Bantam, 1989), as cited in Henry A. Virkler, *Broken Promises* (Dallas: Word Books, 1992), p. 61.

[7]Virkler, *Broken Promises,* p. 60.

[8]Kathleen Fischer Hart and Thomas N. Hart, *The First Two Years of Marriage* (Ramsey, N.J.: Paulist Press, 1983), p. 19.

[9]J. Allan Petersen, *The Myth of the Greener Grass* (Wheaton, Ill.: Tyndale House, 1991), pp. 161-62, 165.

[10]If the encounter was less than six months ago, you need to abstain from sexual relations with your spouse until you get an HIV antibody test administered six full months after the encounter.

[11]In one study of couples who used condoms, three of eighteen partners still became infected. (Cited by Joseph Carey in "Condoms May Not Stop AIDS," *U.S. News & World Report,* Oct. 19, 1987, p. 16.) In another study, one in

ten spouses who used condoms became infected. Among couples who did *not* use condoms, twelve of fourteen spouses became infected (Margaret A. Fischl et al., "Evaluation of Heterosexual Partners, Children, and Household Contacts of Adults with AIDS," *Journal of the American Medical Association,* Feb. 6, 1987, pp. 640-44).

[12]Many of your questions can also be answered by phone. For free medical information, contact the CDC National AIDS Clearinghouse at 800/342-AIDS (Spanish: 800/344-7432; Deaf: 800/243-7889), or your local Red Cross chapter or county public health office. For advice from a Christian perspective, contact Americans For A Sound AIDS/HIV Policy, P.O. Box 17433, Washington, DC 20041; 703/471-7350. There are also a growing number of support groups for Christians with HIV/AIDS. For details, contact the Christian AIDS Services Alliance, P.O. Box 3612, San Rafael, CA 94912.

[13]Willard F. Harley, *His Needs, Her Needs* (Grand Rapids: Revell, 1986), p. 9.

[14]Adapted from Medinger, "For the Married Man," p. 3.

[15]Lois Mowday, *The Snare* (Colorado Springs: NavPress, 1988), p. 92.

Chapter 14: A Vision for the Future

[1]Gerard van den Aardweg, *Homosexuality and Hope* (Ann Arbor, Mich.: Servant, 1985), p. 80.

[2]We agree that discarding the "ex-gay" or "ex-lesbian" label is healthy. However, for the sake of clarity and brevity, we have used such terminology throughout this book as a convenient way of referring to individuals with past homosexual involvement.

[3]Andy Comiskey, "Beyond the Ex-Gay Plateau," *The Exodus Standard* (P.O. Box 2121, San Rafael, CA 94912), Spring 1988, p. 1. Some material in this section is adapted from this article. Used by permission.

[4]Ibid.

[5]Ibid., p. 4.

[6]Taken from the audiotape "Emotional Dynamics Common to Recovery" by Joe Dallas and Jeff Konrad (Exodus International, 1990).

[7]Ibid.

[8]Some material takes from Starla Allen, "Releasing the Woman Within," in *Pursuing Sexual Wholeness Guide* (Lake Mary, Fla.: Creation House, 1988), pp. 172-74. Used by permission.

Appendix A: Answers to Common Pro-Gay Arguments

[1]Derrick Sherwin Bailey, *Homosexuality and the Western Christian Tradition* (Harlow, England: Longmans, Green, 1955). See also John Boswell, *Christianity, Social Tolerance and Homosexuality* (Chicago: University of Chicago Press, 1980), p. 94.

[2]Ronald M. Springett, "What Does the Old Testament Say About Homosexuality?" in *The Crisis of Homosexuality,* ed. J. Isamu Yamamoto (Wheaton, Ill.: Victor Books, 1990), p. 137.

[3]Ibid., p. 138.

[4]John Oswalt, "What the Old Testament Says About Homosexuality," in *Answers to Your Questions About Homosexuality,* ed. Cynthia Lanning (Wilmore, Ky.: Forum Script, Bristol Books, 1988), p. 45.

[5]Ibid.

[6]Ronald M. Springett, "What Does the New Testament Say About Homosexuality?" in *The Crisis of Homosexuality,* p. 151.

[7]Richard F. Lovelace, *Homosexuality: What Should Christians Do About It?* (Old Tappan, N.J.: Revell, 1978, 1984), p. 92.

[8]J. Harold Greenlee, "What the New Testament Says About Homosexuality," in *Answers to Your Questions About Homosexuality,* p. 63.

[9]William Barclay, *The Ten Commandments for Today* (New York: Harper, 1973), p. 154; as cited by Greenlee, p. 61.

[10]Greenlee, "What the New Testament Says," p. 66.

[11]Ibid., p. 67.

[12]Springett, "What Does the New Testament Say," p. 157.

[13]Lovelace, *Homosexuality,* p. 102.

[14]Ibid., p. 103.

[15]John Stott, *Homosexual Partnerships? Why Same-Sex Relationships Are Not a Christian Option* (Downers Grove, Ill.: InterVarsity Press, 1984, 1985), pp. 15-16.

[16]Lovelace, *Homosexuality,* p. 104.